Studies in Education No. 27

Grandma's Attic or Aladdin's Cave:
Museum Education Services for Children

On front cover: *Explorers Week*
holiday programme at Otago Museum.
The brown bear, beloved by children,
was a gift from the British Museum
about a century ago (Photo: John
Darby).

Grandma's Attic or Aladdin's Cave

Museum Education Services for Children

Constance Hall

New Zealand Council
for Educational Research
Wellington, 1981

New Zealand Council
for Educational Research
P.O. Box 3237
Wellington

© NZCER 1981

ISSN 0111-2422
ISBN 0-908567-15-4

Printed by
Deslandes Limited
178–182 Willis Street
Wellington

How are we to know what children derive from museum visits? (Photo: John Buckland).

At the root of most of our troubles as human beings is the lack of any sort of interest at all except for self-preservation. Of what use are any of the proposed panaceas for the preservation of evolved civilization or the maintenance of cultures, if the majority of living people simply don't care? If the education industry does not create people who are interested in the world around them during their one single life, then education is, above all, a failure.

I would contend that museums are the greatest available laboratory for studying the problem of how to create interest and that this problem is central to our survival as people.

Dillon S. Ripley
from *The Sacred Grove*

Contents

'The satisfaction of having time to complete a task'. This child has made his own fish-hook from primitive materials (Photo: John Buckland).

Preface

Work on this report began by reading, from their earliest beginnings, the annual reports of the four metropolitan museums, and by examining their efforts to communicate with children.[1] These brief and factual summaries contained an unexpected record of long and sustained efforts by at least three museum educators who were also museum directors, stimultaneously extending the boundaries of research, the quality of their collections and showing their desire to assist children to experience these joys and satisfactions. Something of the work of two of these men, Sir Gilbert Archey, Director of the Auckland War Memorial Museum (also known as the Auckland Institute and Museum), and Sir Robert Falla, Director of the National Museum, Wellington, is mentioned in this book. The work of Sir William Benham, Professor of Zoology, University of Otago and Curator of the Otago University Museum (now Otago Museum) with teachers and children has largely been forgotten. But records of his research remain, and so does the collection which his successor, Professor Brian J. Marples, described to us when we were students of zoology as the finest collection for teaching comparative anatomy in the Southern Hemisphere. Much of the work of this report has been in acknowledgement of our debt to these men, as well as to others in the past, for the unique heritage their efforts secured for us.

This re-examination of those museum education services established under the supervision of the New Zealand Council for Educational Research has been carried out under their auspices, largely through the initiative and determination of John E. Watson, its Director, who wished to have it recorded. I wish to thank him for his support and also Dr Geraldine McDonald, Assistant Director, whose patience and support have largely sustained these efforts, and Alistair Campbell, Senior Editor, under whose guidance the manuscript has been prepared. The Department of Education granted access to its officers, records and all necessary institutions. Teachers college staffs, district senior inspectors,

1. Held in the Library, National Museum, Wellington.

museum directors and education officers have all been generous with their time and information, and have freely supplied illustrations of their varied activities. The figures on attendance of school classes at museums where there is no education officer have been supplied by Professor K. Thomson, Massey University. Interviews with former education officers, including the four involved in the initial experiments, have been a journey through time. Miss Pat McDonald, Education Officer-in-Chief, Australian Museum, Sydney, helped me extensively with information and advice about services in Australia. To all of these people I wish to extend my sincere thanks.

Generous travelling expenses were provided by NZCER for me to visit all 13 museum education centres in New Zealand, and by the McKenzie Education Foundation for me to visit selected institutions in Australia, thereby making personal interviewing possible and for this I am most grateful.

Constance Hall

Introduction

During the past decade there has been a world-wide movement to re-examine the activities of museums and to consider their social function in relation to the needs of the contemporary world. Containing as they do the material record of man's achievements, they are one of the great cultural assets of our society. Of the three accepted functions of a museum — collection and conservation of objects, research, and education — it is the third which excites the most controversy.

Urgency was given to a re-examination of the role of the museum in society by the attendance explosion, which, in the sixties, appeared to be increasing at a rate faster than that of population growth or of the establishment of new museums. In the Belmont Report[1] commissioned by the President of the United States to examine this phenomeon we read:

> The increase has been so rapid and has reached such a level, that museums now have to turn down requests for service. Yet the times call for a sharp increase in the educational and cultural opportunities which museums are uniquely equipped to provide.

> The increased demands on museums come from all ages and segments of the population, affect not only the institutions in metropolitan centres but those elsewhere, and reflect the dependence on museums of both the disadvantaged and the affluent.

> As far as can be forseen, the factors responsible for the increased demands on museums are likely to continue to prevail indefinitely.

A suggestion that the diverging role of museums is linked to a fundamental change in educational needs comes from Alison Heath,[2] President of the Working Party on Training, ICOM Committee for Education and Cultural Action (CECA), who writes:

> The increasing urbanization of our society is causing a fundamental change in the

1. *Belmont Report*. Published in 1969 by the American Association of Museums. Quoted in *Museums, Imagination and Education: Museums and Monuments, XV* (Paris: Unesco, 1973), p.91.
2. Alison Heath, 'Excursions to Museums, Sites and Monuments as "Sources of Knowledge"', in *Museum*, Vol. XXXI, No. 3 (Paris, 1979), p.210.

educational needs of young people which should be reflected in a development in the role of museums.

When the British education system was first created, children had plenty of first-hand experience of life: the family was a closely knit unit, covering the whole age range. Every aspect of work and recreation was apparent within the local community. On the other hand it was difficult for young people to find out about the world outside their own immediate neighbourhood. Their education was, therefore, based on secondary sources, books, drawings, photographs, etc. Now, television and radio have reinforced the printed word to make this 'other world' more easily accessible, if still at second hand. *It is the direct personal experience that is now more likely to be missing.* (Italics mine)

In line with the re-examination of museums and their educational role in other countries, this survey hopes to provide the first step in a long overdue appraisal of the educational resources of New Zealand museums. Of their many aspects, this report describes only those services for children which are run currently by the Department of Education in 13 museums, together with the history of their development.

1   Current Class Visits to Museums

Although museums have traditionally been oriented towards adults and indeed some major New Zealand museums formerly excluded unaccompanied children from their galleries, for the past 40 years, in the four main museums, classes of school children have been taught during school hours in the public galleries. The buses which bring them have become part of the museum landscape and so have the children's activities, adding colour and interest to an otherwise formal scene. Although museums stand apart from the traditional three-tiered structure of the education system, school children are their privileged visitors with facilities not normally available to adults. They are helped to understand the significance of objects in the collections and are also allowed to handle and examine many of them. As their classes are conducted in the public galleries, parents and visitors are able to watch and listen to the children. The Department of Education has now extended these services to 13 of our many museums. As all develop their programmes according to the strengths of the collections, none is the same as another and no day will be the same as the one before.

The subject areas vary according to the collections, but generally they cover Pre-European Maori, early colonial history, earth sciences, natural sciences and cultures of other parts of the world, principally the Pacific and ancient civilizations. Some have a planetarium or working models of the universe, which are useful for intermediate or secondary classes. Many have furnished historic cottages, schools, churches, clusters of shops or even a whole street representative of their city about 100 years ago, where one can 'shop' and study. The more recently established 'open' or 'live' museums have large complexes of buildings covering housing, transport and technology where study, dramatic learning and real tasks challenging to the children are provided. There are opportunities for bread-making and baking in camp ovens, for sawing and chopping wood, for washing and ironing clothes of their great-grandparents' day with washboards and irons of their time. Most lessons

1

Students from Wellington Teachers College extend a simplified marae *welcome to classes arriving for lessons in the Maori Hall, National Museum (Photo: National Museum).*

centre on objects related to a theme undertaken at school. The topic may have been selected from a list provided by the museum or arranged by discussion between teacher and museum education officer.

The introduction of Maori studies to the teachers colleges has made teachers less dependent on the museums for information on this subject, but the Maori halls of the major museums are those most frequently used (see Figures A1, A2, 'Analysis of Booked Visits to the Auckland War Memorial Museum', Appendix E). The simplified *marae* welcome in front of the Maori meeting house at the National Museum often draws appreciative comments from onlookers, drawn to listen to the simple songs and greetings from the museum education staff and the children in reply. Series of objects may be provided for comparative studies, for example, collections related to Maori fishing may be presented beside Pakeha counterparts so that comparisons can be made. Provision of duplicate artefacts or high quality replicas for handling enable children to experiment with their use, perhaps to play a Maori flute, to generate heat from wooden tools for fire-making, to dress in Maori clothing or to use a Maori drill. Reconstruction of archaeological 'digs' in sandpits provides opportunities for them to assemble a collection of artefacts from which they make their own deductions about another life style. There is now less demand for the teaching of Maori games and pastimes, although these may be taught if requested.

Lessons on natural history fill a need, as many teachers are insecure about this type of teaching. It would seem to have been a problem for a long time. In the annual report of the Otago University Museum (now Otago Museum) in 1915, the curator, Dr William Benham, expressed concern at the poor level of knowledge of natural history and suggested ways in which museums might help to improve this. Teachers and children prefer to observe live animals in association with mounted specimens, but the care of live animals is demanding. They may be used for a limited period of time, as in Taranaki Museum where a topic of this nature is offered for a school term. A lesson on the life history of the eel, for example, used a tank of elvers caught at the local power station, and another of adult eels. The topic 'Introduced Mammals of New Zealand' used small mammals such as mice, rats, guinea pigs and so on, as well as the collection of mounted specimens. Small creatures such as spiders may be handled when mounted in fibreglass, or bees may be observed in temporary sections of a hive with glass walls. Specimens mounted in fibreglass may later be made available for loan to the schools.

Lessons related to other periods of man's history or to other cultures may use mime, role-playing or drama to show the use to which the objects were put. Role-playing is particularly suited to studies of early pioneer life in New Zealand, as in the re-enactment of a school lesson. Dressed in clothes of

3

another era, and seated on forms or school benches in a restored, one-roomed school, the children write on school slates and read the textbooks used by children many years ago. In the report of the education officer, Taranaki Museum, December 1977, Mrs Judy Hoyle writes:

> Perhaps the most popular topic with the children was the schoolroom set up in the museum. They thoroughly enjoyed joining in with the Victorian 'teacher', being put on the dunce's stool and being 'struck' with her very long stick. In fact during the weekends that the schoolroom has been set up we have had many young weekend visitors acting out their Victorian lesson by themselves. The fact that many of our regular weekend visitors come during the weekend of their own volition gives me a great deal of satisfaction; it indicates that the pleasure and interest shown by the children is genuine.

The following sample lesson for young children at a pioneer cottage indicates some of the strategies used by a museum teacher in a lesson of this type. The children were new entrants, 5-6 years of age, whose class teacher wished them to visit the furnished cottage in the museum grounds at Gisborne. A simple theme was chosen to show important differences between early cottages and modern homes, and the children were brought to the museum to 'have a bath'. On reaching the house and exploring the rooms the children could find no bathroom or plumbing, and a problem solving situation was set up. Without a bathroom, how do you have a bath? The ritual of a Saturday night bath in an early New Zealand cottage was then enacted. Objects of special value were not handled by children, but the portable bath could be lifted down from the wall and placed before the fireplace 'to keep warm'. Towels were then spread before the fireplace. With no taps and running water, boilers from the kitchen stove had to be taken to the backyard pump, 'filled' and replaced on the stove. To heat the water, the fuel had to be selected and axes and saws examined, and the use of flints, matches and paper spills for fire-making demonstrated. The children then mimed the carrying of heated water to fill the bath, and examined the old fashioned clothes with their awkward, cloth-covered buttons which had to be undone, while awaiting their turn to be 'washed' in the bath with oddly-smelling homemade soap. During this make-believe several interesting points emerged. The children were horrified to find that the same bath water would have to be used for several people in succession, and were also anxious when the teacher took her turn in the bath which they considered unsuitable for adults. 'You are too big. You're all scrumpled up. It will slosh over.' Without plugs to empty the bath, the water had to be 'bailed' out, carried to the backyard and emptied into the herb garden. Having so much work to do was very strenuous and, by general agreement, next Saturday night was considered quite soon enough to have another bath of this kind.

Teaching in museums has its own problems. The most common is the need for the children to have an adequate view of the exhibits. When a class of 35-40

Bath night at Gisborne Art Gallery and Museum (Photo: Don Millar).

Re-enactment of a Victorian school lesson (Photo: Taranaki Herald).

children is in the care of one museum officer, viewing small objects under glass is almost impossible. The crowding and restricted space leads to an over-formal and over-disciplined atmosphere or else to an unproductive dispersal of interest. One solution is to take the materials from the galleries and use them in the museum classroom. However, important exhibits cannot be removed from public view. Moreover, conducting the lessons entirely in the classroom may prevent the children from entering and learning to use the public galleries. In the metropolitan museums, the single classroom that each one has would have to be used by 2 or 3 classes who are there at the same time but may be studying different topics. These rooms are also some distance from many galleries. By contrast, in the smaller museums, a room, or a reserved gallery area is used successfully in this way, with specially mounted exhibitions from which the children can move readily to explore additional materials in the adjacent public galleries.

A second problem is the limited time for a visit. Classes usually arrive about 9.30 and will commonly spend 1 to 1½ hours studying exhibits related to their theme. A second wave of classes arrives in mid-morning, followed by one or two waves in the afternoon. By mid-afternoon there are no classes left in the museums because the teachers try to return them to their schools before the closing time of 3 p.m.

Both of these problems result in an over-emphasis on verbal explanations of the exhibits with little or no participation by the children. It is possibly the least effective use to be made of these visits.

A standard but controversial method used widely to help to direct the children's observation while spreading the class round the exhibits is the use of question or activity sheets. Most of the present education officers have used them for a while and then abandoned them. Some claim that, rather than direct the children to the objects, they direct them merely to the completion of the activity sheets. They point out that mechanical difficulties such as the rear-rangement of exhibits, problems with labels and the age level to which the sheets are directed detract from their effectiveness. Their value is an open question but children undoubtedly enjoy doing them in a leisure situation. A variation of the activity sheets are the open-ended work cards designed for the Avoncroft Museum of Buildings.[1]

The most widely approved solution is for the children to work in small groups. From 1938-68, groups in the main museums were in the care of teachers college students who were 'posted' there for training. As students have been available only intermittently since then, alternatives have been sought, using volunteers or parents, or with the greater involvement of the

1. *Pterodactyls and Old Lace: Museums in Education*, Schools Council Publication (London: Evans Brothers and Methuen Educational, 1972), pp. 28-30. Also Appendix B, pp.88-90.

class teacher. Volunteers have been used at the Hawkes Bay Art Gallery and Museum since 1949 when a group of people who had been taught about the exhibits by the director, J. Munro, each gave a morning a week to assist with classes. This system still operates with the part-time education officer, N. Bartle, who was appointed in 1970. The National Museum has tried using volunteers, but this is not favoured by the New Zealand Educational Institute (NZEI). The Museum of Transport and Technology (MOTAT) involves parents as well as students, when these are available. Booklets for the use of the parents who accompany the classes are sent out to the school with the materials for class preparation.

Their group system works like this. After an introduction from the education officer, using handling materials, the class moves out into the museum complex and breaks up into groups to view the exhibits. It is the class teacher's job to order the change-over so that all the groups have a chance to see the different exhibits. Meanwhile, each parent remains at the same building, whether it be the potter's cottage, the old school, the church and so on. They assist the children in tasks assigned to direct their observation and also help to answer their questions. The method appears to be successful in catering both for the group situation and for the participation and enjoyment of the parents whose interest and confidence grow with experience[2]

The small group has many advantages. The children can see more readily, can handle objects as they are being discussed without a long wait, and can ask questions more freely and develop discussion. Criticisms of these arrangements are usually concerned with the degree of skill and knowledge the helpers will have. Their knowledge of the collections may be more limited than that of the education officers, and so usually will be their experience in teaching children and in helping them to make their own discoveries. A balance must therefore be determined between the advantages and disadvantages of this method.

Although few classes of primary school children conduct their own class visits to the museum, a class of children of high ability from Cobham Intermediate School, guided by their teacher, J. Paul, was observed in the course of such a study on the Antarctic at Canterbury Museum. Discussion at school and the selection of various areas for study — beauty, explorers, adaptation, and so on — was followed by a visit of the group leaders to the museum to examine the range of exhibits shown to them by the education officers. These leaders were then required to visit the museum again during the weekend with their parents, to show them the materials, and to discuss the ways in which they might be used. The visit of the whole class then followed, and their behaviour

2. Stafford M. Waterman,'Museums as Educational Partners', in *AGMANZ News,* Auckland,Vol. 8, No. 2 (May 1977), pp. 21-4.

in the galleries was most interesting to watch. They appeared relaxed, quiet and purposefully intent on their own line of interest. Some grouped and re-grouped as they worked together, while some worked independently, using a range of recording devices from tape recorders and cameras to notes and sketches. Their teacher, who remained nearby, was quietly consulted from time to time. The effectiveness of this method was marked and appeared to reach an ideal in the way in which the children were using the museum for their own personal interests and enrichment.

'The small group has many advantages' (Photo: National Museum).

All museums provide materials for the children to handle, and this is regarded as the most important service which, as a rule, they alone can provide. To understand an object fully, it may be necessary to handle it. A stone age tool, for example, may appear to be only a chipped piece of stone, but once it is handled and one's fingers fit into its grooves and hollows, it may be recognized for what it is. This can be an exciting moment of discovery and may also lead to a feeling of empathy for the person who made it. The importance of this experience is the central theme of a valuable book on museum teaching, *Educating in Five Dimensions*,[3] but it has also often been emphasized by later writers. The primitive, satisfying experience of touch may be in itself the necessary catalyst to crystallize a learning or an emotional experience. In writing of this, Duncan F. Cameron, an expert on museum communication, states:

> Those who have worked in museums know beyond doubt that the communication of ideas through real things can be so intense and intimate an experience for the child that the picture image, the word symbol, the model or replica and the screen image of film and television become pale shadows.[4]

Films and visual aids are used much less than they were. In the 1940s few schools had film projectors and the National Film Library was just being formed. Museums, which were among the first to have 16mm projectors and which held collections of their own films, formerly used these extensively. But, as most schools now have their own projectors, or have ready access to them, museums make little use of them except to show films which may not be available to the general public, for example, some bird films, or films of aborigine life which the museums may happen to hold.

Lessons are not always confined to the museum buildings. In some centres, trips led by the education officers can be arranged to visit *pa* sites, Maori meeting houses, historical buildings and cemeteries. The National Museum provides information and tapes for using on a variety of historical walks around the city. After a visit to Hawkes Bay Art Gallery and Museum to study the early history of the district, a departing class is given notes on the historical features of the Old Taupo Road to use on their homeward journey. Gisborne Art Gallery and Museum takes the children by bus on a tour of the city to look at a sequence of historic buildings. Here, the siting of the oldest cottage on the museum grounds, beside the museum building which is the most modern in Gisborne, provides an appropriate start and finish to the tour.

As activities require more time than the usual lesson period, there is a growing demand for longer visits of half or whole days. These are now being

3. H.W. Beaumont, *Educating in Five Dimensions* (Wellington: A.H. and A.W. Reed, 1960), p. 10. This is now, unfortunately, out of print.
4. Duncan F. Cameron, 'A Viewpoint: The Museum as a Communications System and its Implications for Museum Education', in *Curator*, New York, Vol. XI, No. 1 (1968), pp. 33-40.

'The primitive, satisfying experience of touch' (Photo: National Museum).

adopted by most museums, although it means that fewer classes may be accommodated. But the satisfaction for the children in learning a skill or in having time to complete their task is thought to outweigh the advantages of more frequent visits. Two museums have special provision for extended visits. At Gisborne Art Gallery and Museum, an annual two-day residential school is held where children work on a theme such as 'The Maori and the Kumara', with time to dig the hole, construct the frame and to thatch a kumara pit, to carve their own pumice bowls, plait food baskets, dig and cook their own kumara, to listen to and dramatize the legends. There is satisfaction in having time and guidance to complete some task, such as making and flying a raupo kite, scaling and gutting a fish with primitive implements before cooking it over a driftwood fire; time to examine weapons and plan strategies, to visit an actual *pa* site to study its defences and to stage one's own battle on a nearby hill. Additional staff and experts assist the education officer to run these courses.

A longer period of up to a week is available throughout the year at Otago Museum where a complex of classrooms, film room, activity area and lunch area is available for classes working under their own teachers. A full and detailed work plan is prepared by each teacher beforehand, time-tabling in films, sessions with education officers, professional museum staff and outside experts at specific times. These classes operate concurrently with visits of shorter duration by other schools. Most of these classes are usually from intermediate schools, but an interesting week was spent some time ago by a group of new entrants under their teacher Mrs C. Stringer on the theme 'The Jungle'. A large fishing net hung in the classroom, which was reserved for the class for the week, as a framework for the creation of a jungle of flowers, leaves, birds, insects and animals. Different museum specimens were brought in at intervals, or were visited in the galleries. Language, music, drama, art and such activities as the teacher wished, could be used freely. The parents of children engaged in these extended visits participate in the final day when creative work is displayed and performances are given. This also gives the museum staff an opportunity to see the creative work produced as a result of the visit.

Many classes send back examples of work done after a short visit, and some museums feature these, particularly Nelson Provincial Museum which is in a new building in a new area, and shrewdly draws attention to itself by listing in newsletters the names of children whose work is on display. Creative work is a normal and spontaneous expression of the feelings a stimulating visit has aroused. As D.V. Proctor says, the children's records are often wonderful and varied, and also often show their willingness to come back and find out more, or to go elsewhere to discover further worlds of learning.[5]

5. D.V. Proctor, 'Museums — Teachers, Students, Children', in *Museums, Imagination and Education: Museums and Monuments*, XV (Paris: Unesco, 1973), pp. 23–9.

Few museums offer activities for children outside the usual school hours, but an exception is the Manawatu Museum, where children are encouraged to visit the museum in the lunch hour to learn to use a collection of old printing presses. The culmination of a course in printing where they learn to set up type and use the presses will be the production of posters, labels for the display cases and information sheets to send out to the schools, or posters for their classroom. The children take pride in their work, and take considerable care to see that their spelling is appropriate. This museum also offers courses in museum conservation, teaching children to care for the collections of the museum. The knowledge that their work will be accepted, and that their skill and care are necessary for the continued preservation of these valued objects, helps to build their self-confidence.

Bringing kumara to their newly constructed storage pit. Residential school at Gisborne Art Gallery and Museum (Photo: Don Millar).

2   Where It All Began

Planning for museums came early in the history of European settlement of New Zealand. By 1871 museums were open in Nelson, Auckland, Wellington, Canterbury, Otago and Southland, long before the first art gallery opened in 1888. Since then the numbers of art galleries and museums have proliferated. When the Carnegie experiments were mounted in 1937 there were 18 museums. This number grew to 38 in 1958, to more than 80 in 1966, and to 116 in 1977. As the early curators were building up their collections they were also naming and identifying local flora and fauna, and their crowded display cases reflected an emphasis on systematics, as well as the desire to collect and display as many as possible of the wonders of nature. This type of display, modelled largely on museums of Victorian England showed little change until, in the 1930s, two outside influences combined powerfully to alter the public image of our museums.

The first was the visit of S.F. Markham in 1933 from the Museums Association of Great Britain in association with the Carnegie Corporation of New York, in the course of a survey of the museums and art galleries of the British Empire. In *A Report on the Museums and Art Galleries of Australia and New Zealand to the Carnegie Corporation of New York,* S.F. Markham gave us high praise for the quality of our institutions, ahead of comparable states or provinces in South Africa, Ireland, Canada and Australia. He writes: 'Museum and art gallery movement owes little to Government but a great deal to thousands of enlightened and public-spirited citizens.'[1] Auckland War Memorial Museum was described as 'the most beautiful and best arranged south of the line' and 'Wanganui has almost the finest art gallery and library for a town of its size anywhere in the Empire'.

In the field of educational work the laurels were distributed very sparsely. Markham said:

Many museums in New Zealand have been content to follow at a distance the lead

1. S.F. Markham and W.R.B. Oliver, *A Report on the Museums and Art Galleries of New Zealand to the Carnegie Corporation of New York* (London: Museums Association, 1933), p.95.

set by Europe and America. Most museums offer facilities for school visits and in one or two cases the curator or his assistant acts as guide lecturer to the school.[2]

Auckland Museum gave lectures to school teachers; Dominion Museum to school classes; only Auckland had circulating loan material; there was no attempt to establish school museums as offshoots of central museums; there was no link with WEA, the Plunket Society, Home Extension Services, agricultural shows or other educational forces of New Zealand.

> In fact the general attitude of one or two New Zealand curators seems to be that they must never look outside the doors of a museum unless it be to secure new specimens. Few curators play that bold, vigorous part in the educational or cultural life of the town such as they play in many American or British cities, while two of them are in fact almost museum recluses to be found daily at their museum office possibly engaged in some work connected with the particular science in which they are interested, but oblivious to the fact that there is a world outside their doors that has never been taught to appreciate museums.[3]

> It is indeed on the educational side that many New Zealand museums like Australian museums are at their weakest; but we hope that the time will come when New Zealand curators will begin to turn their attention to these problems and show that New Zealand can lead the world in visual education as in so many other branches of social activity.[4]

Not all museum curators were oblivious to the outside world but most efforts had been intermittent. Most museums had at times provided services for schools, and a comment in the Otago Museum report for 1905 by Dr Benham about the unscheduled, unplanned visit of school classes shows that common problems have always occurred. The history of educational work in New Zealand museums has been well documented by Dr R.C. Cooper, Assistant Director, Auckland War Memorial Museum in a paper, 'The Role of Museums in Education in New Zealand', presented at the Australian Unesco seminar on 'The Role of Museums in Education', Sydney, in 1966. Dr Cooper, who must have attended some lectures at the Dominion Museum as a pupil, comments: 'My memories are of large classes crowded into a small room, with no chance to handle the material shown and a final wild rush to see the tuatara, lizards and other attractions before catching the tram back to school.' These classes were conducted by the museum staff, who also ran broadcasts to schools from 1935 until 1940.

It was Auckland Museum under the directorship of Dr (Sir Gilbert) Archey who, as early as 1929, had developed a schools service department, which has continued to function since then. From this emerged the pattern of educational work used as a blueprint for activities which developed later in the four largest museums. The success of this work was due largely to Sir Gilbert and Dr (Sir

2. *Ibid.,* p. 101.
3. *Ibid.,* p. 102.
4. *Ibid.,* p. 104.

14

Robert) Falla, education officer on the staff of the museum from 1930. Both of these men had been trained and served as teachers. From the range of activities developed at this museum came a number of developments: the loan display case system, classes for children and teachers college students, children's clubs, competitions with prizes for natural history essays and displays, classes for blind children, activity sheets and educational broadcasts. Division of the classes into small groups was considered essential, and, to do this, museum staff were deployed from other departments. Work for the blind and handicapped was developed intensively and considered of great importance. Children were encouraged to handle museum material, and lessons were developed around ideas and things that children could continue to develop on their own. A close liaison developed with the teachers colleges whose students were brought in for classes, and this became closer in 1934 when, with the closing of the teachers training colleges, one of the college science lecturers was seconded to the museum staff.

An important influence on the educational activities of our museums was the visit to New Zealand in 1935 of Dr F.P. Keppel, President of the Carnegie Corporation, to hold discussions on possible assistance to museums and art galleries for educational work. In the following year he made a grant of $50,000, which was administered by the New Zealand Council for Educational Research. The developments which followed were the work of many hands and minds throughout the country. A record of the three years of experimentation which followed through 1938-40 has been documented by H.C. McQueen in *Education in New Zealand Museums.* [5]

On the recommendations of a special advisory committee set up after Dr Keppel's visit, a five-point plan was accepted, of which the first was the establishment of a schools service in the four metropolitan museums, two in the North Island and two in the South Island, with the appointment to them of trained teachers as education officers. What developed could be called a national scheme of experimentation involving both museums and educational authorities.

The principles on which the work was to be based were clearly defined:

1. *Their task was to use the museum and its resources for the benefit of children.* Hence, the activities of the museum officers included work with children out of school hours, after school, during weekends and holidays, as well as with organized school classes during school hours. Children's clubs were established with lasting effect.

2. *Children were to be encouraged to see the museum as a place for exploration, so*

5. H.C. McQueen, *Education in New Zealand Museums:* An Account of Experiments Assisted by the Carnegie Corporation of New York (Wellington: NZCER, 1942).

classes were to be taken in the museum galleries, and not in separate classrooms.
The upshot was that the flustered custodians were to become all too used to sticky finger marks on glass cases as well as scuffed floors, but, also, significant changes were required in museum display and presentation to make them suitable for children. Although somewhat sceptical to begin with, museum staff quickly discovered the favourable reaction of the public to their new arrangements. Brighter colours, simpler displays, lower cases, clearer, simple, informative labels became the order of the day.

3. *Children were to be taken round the museum in small groups.* To bring this about, four students from the local teachers colleges were allocated to each museum for periods of four weeks. This meant 6-8 children for each student.

4. *Children were to be allowed to handle museum objects.* Possibly this brought most heartache to some museum staffs at the start. The sight of children operating a priceless Maori drill in the museum galleries was to many a tremendous shock. Yet 40 years later the drills are still working, the floors have not been undermined, and little damage has been caused as a result of allowing children to feel, handle, smell and explore some of the treasured objects around them.

5. *The museums were to operate a system of loan material for out-of-town schools.* Accordingly, duplicate or replica material was arranged in small portable cases for circulation mainly within the Education Board district where the museum was located.

It is only in retrospect that the significance of these clear guidelines becomes apparent. The museum officers were left free to operate and develop their activities around the institution and collections to which they were attached, and to serve the needs of the communities in which they were located. They were not expected to conform to any predetermined pattern.

As McQueen[6] points out, radical changes were forced on the museums themselves by these initiatives. Before 1938 unaccompanied children had been denied access to some of these museums, yet after that date leisure-time visits were actively encouraged by the provision of special exhibits, museum trails, games, and so on. These attendances and the swelling numbers of children in class visits during school hours forced museum staffs, from directors down to the cleaners, to accept the more lively atmosphere of these erstwhile formal and even oppressive institutions. Sweeping changes in museum displays encouraged by concurrent Carnegie-funded experiments at the Auckland Institute and Museum by Miss Olwyn Rutherford (Mrs G. Turbott) and at Otago Museum by Miss L.A. Daff and Molly Macalister were further extended by a

6. *Ibid.*, pp. 10-11.

scheme for the exchange of special displays between museums. These stimulated more varied and colourful displays of much greater public appeal. Techniques were also demonstrated and improved by the teachings of Mr Frank Tose of California, a specialist in museum techniques for display and reproduction, whose visit to New Zealand in 1937 was financed by the Carnegie Corporation.

Main Hall, Wanganui Public Museum in the 1890s. Such displays, largely modelled on the museums of Victorian England, were still seen up to the 1930s in New Zealand (Photo: Alexander Turnbull Library).

As Bernard Smyth[7] points out, the gift of money by the Carnegie Corporation of New York to stimulate educational activities at the four metropolitan museums in 1938 was a turning point which led the larger museums to their present important role in the community, changing their formal image into one of leisure-time recreation centres.

The Second World War was to have a devastating effect on museums, both during the experimental years and immediately afterwards. The National Museum, taken over for military purposes, remained closed to the public for over seven years, from June 1942 to September 1949. Only the loan cases continued to circulate. By 1942 the three remaining education officers were on active service and the newly established organizations were in the hands of other teachers largely unfamiliar with this work. In surviving this set-back, the museum education service demonstrated the effectiveness of the planning and evaluation which had gone firstly into the assessment of the pilot work in Auckland and in the subsequent three experimental years.

Early in 1941 the Department of Education took over the responsibility for the school service work, which has continued to operate under its guidance since then. At the final conference of those involved in the experiments, a discussion took place between the four museum directors, their education officers, officers of NZCER and of the Department of Education, in order to exchange views informally. It is interesting to see the aims put forward then on which there was general agreement, and which continued to guide and moderate this work for the next 30 years or so:[8]

(1) To make the educational facilities of the museums available to all adults and children, for both formal and informal education.

(2) To widen the work of museums to include hobbies and interests.

(3) To develop interest in the museum itself and to see it recognized by everybody as an educational institution.

(4) To bring children into contact with objects relevant to the understanding of man's history.

(5) To provide teaching material for use in the ordinary work of teachers.

(6) To show teachers how to use the museum and the resources which were being developed to meet their needs.

(7) To teach children how to use the museum to answer their questions and solve their problems.

7. Bernard W. Smyth, *The Role of Culture in Leisure Time in New Zealand*, Series: Studies and Documents on Cultural Policies (Paris: Unesco, 1973), pp. 21-3.
8. NZCER Museums Trust Conference on Education in Museums, Wellington, New Zealand, 12 March 1941 (mimeo, NZCER).

(8) To teach children how to use and enjoy the museum so that when they are adults they will maintain and develop their interests through it.

(9) To make everyone feel at home in a museum.

(10) To make the museum a place where children would come to *do* things in a properly equipped workroom for use by both children and adults.

(11) To reflect local and environmental differences in each museum, and to encourage diversity in methods and practices in the museums so that the experimental aspect of the work would continue.

(12) To recognize the needs of country schools and children for museum experiences.

(13) To attach professional teachers to the museum staffs as education officers. While not actually staff members, the museum directors invited them to so regard themselves.

(14) To emphasize the importance of the association of the education officers with the teachers colleges, to whose staffs they were attached. In the past, teachers had not realized or understood the resources of the museum, so a relationship with the teachers colleges was developed to give future teachers a knowledge of the aims and resources of the museum.

This has been the only point in the history of educational work in our museums when general principles were defined by consensus between museum directors and education authorities. The provision for individual freedom of development as well as foundations on which to work had both a stabilizing and a stimulating effect on the developing education services. The period of experimentation was over and the period of growth could begin. Out of this had emerged a situation which now intimately involved three types of educational institution — the museum, the school, the teachers college — in a unique combination to promote museum work with children.

(1) *The museums* from whom the initial impetus had come. They were looking for an extension of their function as educational institutions within the community, a function previously unrecognized by the majority of their visitors. This was now largely taken over by professional teachers known as education officers. Responsibility for their appointment, salaries, some operating costs, and a supply of cases for loan materials, was taken over by the Department of Education. The museums supplied accommodation, materials for teaching, materials for portable displays, and part of the running costs. For administrative purposes, the Department of Education attached the education officers to the staffs of the teachers colleges whose students were posted to the museums for training. Most of their work lay mainly in museums of which they were not staff members. Good personal relationships were imperative if the work was to be successful. Directors had no authority over the education officers except the power to prohibit undesirable activities. The work of the education officers did not affect educational activities being carried out by members of the museum staffs, some of whom continued to operate a number of children's clubs.

(2) *The schools* for whom the majority of the services were provided. They were invited to use museum services either for lessons on museum topics, or for assistance in taking their own lessons with their classes in the museums. Lessons were often associated with films and visual aids which were largely unknown in schools at that time. Loan cases of exhibits, leaflets, illustrations, and so on, were also provided.

(3) *The teachers colleges* to whose staffs the education officers were attached. This association was considered desirable for two main reasons. There was a need to educate teachers in the use of the museum and its resources, and so, as well as providing in-service courses for trained teachers, student teachers were shown the educational possibilities of museums and how to use them effectively. They were also used to reduce the numbers of children in each group while viewing things in the galleries.

From this promising beginning it is surprising to find that for almost 30 years little significant change took place; the four centres have continued to operate on basically similar lines. While attendance figures generally rose steadily with the rising school population, they continued to vary, without significant increase, at between 17-25 percent of the total school population (see Table A1). In each centre, staffing increased in 1942 to two teachers, and at different times from 1943 to an art technician as well, and all were paid by the Department of Education. A technical assistant was appointed to the Auckland War Memorial Museum in 1949, and one to the National Museum in 1957. As child numbers rose, so did the numbers of students, until from 12-20 were allocated each month to each museum (see Tables A6, A7). While more emphasis was placed on student training, work with children out of school hours virtually ceased. The description of this training, published by ICOM in *Museums and Teachers*, 1956, has been widely quoted. Only in the past 10 years have significant changes occurred:

(1) In 1965 for administrative purposes, museum education staff were transferred from the teachers college staffs to local, mainly normal schools.

(2) From 1967 with the introduction of Three Year Training in the teachers colleges, a different method of using schools for practise teaching virtually ended what was by then a traditional relationship. Although three of the four museums are still used for training, the intermittent pattern of student postings has forced their education officers to develop alternative teaching methods, while continuing to meet the demand from schools for attendance of large numbers of school classes.

(3) Part-time or full-time teachers have been appointed to an additional nine museums, four of which combine with art galleries, though the teachers' duties do not extend to this area. One museum (MOTAT) is of a kind usually described as a 'live' or 'open' museum with numerous buildings grouped in a large area. Three of these new centres also train student teachers at times.

Trained teachers are now located in the following museums in New Zealand:

Auckland War Memorial Museum*, 3 teachers, 1 art technician.
Museum of Transport and Technology (MOTAT), Auckland, 1 teacher, full-time since 1973.
Gisborne Art Gallery and Museum, part-time teacher since 1973.
Hawkes Bay Art Gallery and Museum, Napier, a volunteer service for schools operated from 1949. Part-time teacher since 1970.

* Denotes museum involved in original experimental work, 1938-40.

Waikato Art Museum, Hamilton, part-time teacher since 1971, full-time since 1978.

Taranaki Museum, New Plymouth, part-time teacher since 1966, full-time from 1970.

Manawatu Museum, Palmerston North, part-time teacher since 1974, full-time from 1978.

National (formerly Dominion) Museum,* Wellington, 2 teachers, 1 art technician.

Wanganui Public Museum, part-time teacher from 1968, full-time from 1969.

Nelson Provincial Museum, Stoke, part-time teacher since 1974.

Canterbury Museum,* Christchurch, 3 teachers, one of whom is seconded annually, 1 art technician.

Otago Museum,* Dunedin, 2 teachers, 1 art technician. One teacher worked on an experimental basis at the Otago Early Settlers Museum in 1979. This was withdrawn in 1980.

Southland Museum (combined with art gallery), Invercargill, part-time teacher since 1967.

Most appointments to new centres have been made in the past five years and pressures are coming from a number of areas for further extensions. Some figures taken from the questionnaires sent out to all museums by Professor K. Thomson of Massey University in 1978 show that in 1977 substantial numbers of school children visited museums which had no education officer, and some of these were:

Otago Early Settlers Museum: 10 classes, 286 children and an additional holiday programme

Arrowtown Lakes District Centennial Museum: 29 classes, 1,500 children.

South Canterbury Centennial Museum. Timaru: 36 classes, 1,240 children.

Pleasant Point Railway and Historical Museum: 25 classes, 1,120 children.

Langlois-Eteveneaux House and Museum, Akaroa: 35 classes, 1,200 children.

O'Kains Bay Maori and Colonial Museum: 15 classes, 450 children.

West Coast Historical Museum, Hokitika: 36 classes, 1221 children.

West Coast Historical and Mechanical Society, Shantytown: 50 classes, 2,000 children.

Tokomaru Steam Museum: 10 classes, 400 children.

Taihape District and Historical Museum and Society: 25 classes, 750 children.

Onga Onga Old School Museum: 3 classes, 120 children.

Te Amorangi Trust Museum, Holden's Bay, Rotorua: 722 classes, 14,000 children.

Rotorua City Museum: 110 classes, 4,400 children.

* Denotes museum involved in original experimental work, 1938-40.

Tauranga District Museum (Historic Village): 142 classes, 5,230 children.
Helensville and District Pioneer Museum: 10 classes, 300 children.
Clapham Clock Museum, Whangarei: 62 classes, 2,015 children.
Rewa's Village, Kerikeri: 50+ classes, 4,500 children.
Far North Regional Museum, Kaitaia: 12 classes, 376 children.

While this is not a complete list of all museums, these totals, in addition to the 262,761 children who attended the 13 staffed centres, indicate an attendance of over 303,869 children in school classes visiting museums in 1977. The figures are certain to include the same classes on several visits, but analysis to define these is not possible from these figures. It is clear that this is a natural growth which appears to be paralleled in other countries.

In Australia the growth as shown by the growing number of education officers has been phenomenal. At the seminar in Sydney on the *Role of Museums in Education*[9] in 1966, only 7 full-time education officers were known in the country; by the 1971 conference there were 55; by 1975, approximately 100 officers were employed full-time, and many others on a voluntary or part-time basis. Records of a seminar *New Directions in Education* (1975)[10] show that when their service experience was analysed there were few who had more than three years experience and, before the conference, the service mean was approximately 18 months.

9. *The Role of Museums in Education,* Australian Unesco Seminar (Sydney: Australian National Advisory Committee for Unesco, 1966).
10. *New Directions in Museum Education,* National Conference on Museum Education (Adelaide: Australian National Advisory Committee for Unesco, 1975).

Scaling and gutting fish with primitive implements for their lunch (Photo: Don Millar).

Digging kumara with replica Maori tools they have made (Photo: Don Millar).

3   Why Museums Are Used for School Children

Clear answers are needed to the apparently simple question, 'What can museums do for education which nobody else can do?' While many statements of aims for museums exist, as Barry Wells, Superintendent of Social Studies, Education Department of Western Australia, pointed out during a forum on 'Museum Education as I See it: A Personal Viewpoint' at the MEAA Conference in Perth, 1979,[1] in practice clear statements outlining the educational aims of particular museums are the exception rather than the rule, and this lack of clear definition of purpose seems to be a major weakness in museum education programmes.

As Wells further states:

> As I see it, education in museums is more a reflex action to pressures applied from schools and some community groups, than a considered and structured programme in which initiatives have been developed by professional educators and museum officers.

> Responsibility for the clear definition of goals and the development of long-term strategies to achieve these goals must be accepted by the people who are best equipped to manage this important task.

> Much closer cooperation between museum specialists and educators [is needed] so that a high degree of integration of the activities of museums and educational institutions can occur.

Although these comments may have been aimed at the museums of Australia, they are undoubtedly valid criticisms if applied to our museums, and attempts to define policy goals and strategies by which they may be realized have seldom been sustained. The key to the future success of museum services may well lie in the cooperation of museum specialists and educators on educational objectives.

The first successful attempt to do this was in 1941 when museums, education officers and officers of the Department of Education combined to offer

---

1. *Museum Education in a Changing World*, MEAA Conference (Perth, 1979), pp. 40–1.

guidelines for the new services (see Chapter 2). Of later efforts to re-examine policies and strategies, the most purposeful and sustained attempt came from a special Advisory Committee on Museum Education set up in Dunedin in 1969 by S.E.A. Breach, DSI, Otago Education Board. As Breach pointed out, no widely accepted approach to museum education had been put forward, and he suggested that ideas should be proposed for examination and experimentation. The purposes of this committee as outlined in the Annual Report of the Otago Museum 1969-70 were as follows:

(1) To establish the function of the museum education services in primary and intermediate education today and to indicate any means by which it might extend and strengthen the services it offers.

(2) To explore ways in which the interdependence of the museum and the education service might be developed and consolidated in the interests of the children of Otago and elsewhere.

(3) To consider the role that the museums and the education service best play in primary teacher training.

(4) To investigate current practices in museum education throughout the world in order to consider and evaluate new ideas that might improve the service provided by the Otago Museum for children in the province.

Records of the work of this committee are held at Otago Museum in the Education Section. The move to use some of the relatively spacious areas available for education in this museum for in-depth studies for classes for up to a week at a time has been one of the successful strategies developed through this committee.

Museums differ so widely that it is unlikely that tightly defined aims would be appropriate for general use. In Great Britain and Northern Ireland, as Victoria Airey points out:

The aims of museum education services are very flexible indeed, and deliberately so. In a profession which is still developing rapidly, where the museum has so much potential to offer, and where educational ideas and technology are constantly changing, educational activities within the museum must be ready to provide a great variety of methods through which people can receive insight into and enjoyment of the collections.[2]

The need to decide whether or not museums should be part of the educational system in the first place was emphasized by Unesco in its Final Report on an *International Symposium of Museums in the Contemporary World* held in Paris, 1969, which states:

It would be desirable to define the exact social function of the museum at the present time:

(1) As an institution forming an integral part of the education system and able to play an important role in the sectors of science, education and culture: or

2. *Museums and Children:* Monographs on Education, Ulla Keding Olofsson, editor (Paris: Unesco, 1979), p.149.

(2) As a specific institution designed for the benefit of individual enrichment, providing selective or comprehensive information, so contributing towards man's development and his integration in the national and universal community.[3]

In summarizing the discussion, three different viewpoints are recorded:

(1) The idea of making museums a part of the education system should be rejected, not because museums are not concerned with education but because they achieve their educational aims by methods entirely different from those used in traditional education. The museum, like the concert hall, the theatre or the playground, must remain a private environment for a personal and intimate experience.

(2) ... The influence of any cultural experience is liable to be fleeting and superficial unless backed by the systematic and continuing action of schools and universities. The museum can only develop the appreciative faculties of visitors who come in organized groups, with the social discipline that that implies.

(3) The visual culture that can be acquired in museums is the necessary complement to school education and makes a contribution to general culture.

Obviously the needs of each country will differ and not all will accept the same solution. But the exercise of self-examination and evaluation is an important one.

In New Zealand the first strategy, to ally the museums with the education system and to cater for school classes, has been developed, and provision for the individual experience has been thrust aside by the demands of the larger group. Lacking experience of children visiting museums on a voluntary basis, we do not know which makes the better use of our resources. Our museum school services have been developed for four decades both in quantity and in the quality of work done, yet we are little further in understanding which is the most effective way to use this storehouse of knowledge. There are world-wide trends to use museums increasingly for school classes and Hans L. Zetterberg, in *Museums and Adult Education*,[4] states that by now more that half of all visits to museums in the world are made by school classes. It is necessary to look closely at children to try to find out what coming into contact with museum artefacts means to them, as well as examine the benefits to both schools and museums of this activity.

Most museums encourage the visits of school classes for widely accepted reasons related to their need to communicate with the public. In speaking of school service work, J.L.J. Wilson summarizes some of these advantages when he states:

3. *International Symposium on Museums in the Contemporary World*, Final Report (Paris: Unesco, 1969).
4. Hans L. Zetterberg, *Museums and Adult Education* (Augustus Kelly for ICOM with the help of Unesco, 1969), p.8.

For many reasons it is far easier for museums to undertake some expansion of their educational work with children and schools than it is to do so with adults. School children are a far more homogenous group; they can be brought to the museum in age groups; their curricula are known and specific; their teachers can be consulted and help in the planning of educational work at the museum and prepare and follow up what should be shown to them, and the methods of talks, demonstrations and so on can be defined fairly precisely. If the museum is in a position to have its own educational staff, specializing in this work, as a few in this country [Australia] are, a considerable diversity of direct as well as indirect educational activity can be organized for this potentially very large audience.[5]

Criticisms of such visits are usually directed at the scope rather than the availability of these programmes, if their purpose appears merely to supplement the work of the school. At the same conference, T.A. Hume pointed out that there could be a tendency to miss the vital opportunity such a visit provided to emphasize the different atmosphere of the museum if programmes are limited only to the watertight compartments of the classroom, transposed into the museum. He said:

We are guilty of a deadly sin if we do anything to destroy the magic of the museum wonderland — the magic which holds all the elements necessary for stimulation of their curiosity and interest, and the spawning of their imagination.[6]

This curiosity and these feelings of wonder and excitement appear to be aroused fairly readily in young or in handicapped children, particularly when they are allowed to handle the artefacts. It is more difficult to arouse similar interest in children at the secondary school level. Peter Cox, Principal of Dartington College of Arts in Totnes, Devon, comments on this, and in reading his statement that 'only the occasional student arrives at our college having retained this sense of wonder and excitement';[7] one is tempted at first to blame the school system, a traditional whipping boy for such purposes, but the problem appears to be so widespread that is is more likely to be related to increasing maturity. Certainly it is harder to arouse these feelings in adults.

Another reason why museums welcome school classes is that many children return to the museum with their parents, acting as interpreter to the collections. The importance of this to our museums must be emphasized. It is widely accepted that the best way of making collections intelligible is through a sympathetic guide, and the enthusiasm of these children is claimed by all museums to have increased attendances, particularly at weekends, to a marked degree. School classes also bring in children from all sectors of the community

5. J.L.J. Wilson, 'Museums in Adult Education', in *The Role of Museums in Education* (Sydney: Australian Unesco Seminar, 1966), p. 124.
6. T.A. Hume, 'Museums and Education in the United Kingdom', *ibid.*, p. 9.
7. Peter Cox, 'The Museum and Youth', papers from the Ninth Conference of ICOM, pp. 137-43. This article also contains interesting experimental approaches used to arouse the interest of pupils of secondary school age in aspects of art, restoration and in environmental studies.

and this may be crucial for those from poorer homes, who, according to surveys in America and Europe, do not readily visit museums.

Services for school classes are so widespread that almost all our museums provide them, even small institutions where there is no paid curator. It has not been possible to visit many of these, but, of those that have been visited, Patea Museum has been chosen as an example of a small, recently established museum of quality, staffed by voluntary committee members. Within two years of its establishment it had well-presented exhibits related to early and contemporary Maori communities, early pioneer material with emphasis on farm machinery, and so on. Its relationship with the local school was close enough to encourage the teachers to seek help from committee members to understand the collections in preparation for a class visit conducted by each teacher who had access to the museum through a key held at the school. Such situations are repeated in many small museums throughout the country, consciously aiming at the needs of children through the schools, and, through them, of their parents.

On their part, the schools gain access to collections of authentic objects which can excite children and stimulate their curiosity and learning to a marked degree. Surveys in America and Great Britain on the educational potential of their museums end with the same word, 'awestruck'. In the report by the education authorities in Great Britain we read:

> We are overwhelmed with the quantity of exhibits which our museums possess... and to which they are constantly adding. To conserve is the museum's first priority; to educate and entertain is a close second. To conserve for future generations whilst ignoring the present generation would be absurd. To constitute museums formally as institutions responsible for the provision of education would be administratively cumbersome, educationally dubious and could diminish the delight of the millions who visit our museums each year. To ignore their resources as tools for the educationalist is incomprehensible.[8]

While a large body of information has been published on the value of museum education to the individual, few statements define this adequately because of the complexity of the reaction. Writing on this problem, Renée Marcousé says:

> The assessment of the value of museum services to the individual is no easy matter — a talk or essay may well show how far a presentation of fact has gone, but there is no generally acceptable measure of emotional responses — and a very grave danger in attempting to translate it into another medium — into words.
> What we see, the emotions aroused, the associations induced, these make up our experience. It is immediate but it is not simple. The process has many implications; it is related to our tactile sense, to visual memory, to imagination, to past experience, to our predilections, to the ability to discriminate and to our sense of values.[9]

8. *Museums in Education:* Education Survey, No. 12 (London: Department of Education and Science, HMSO, 1971), Introduction, p. vii.
9. Renée Marcousé, 'Animation and Information', Appendix D, in *Museums and Education* by Hans L. Zetterberg, *op.cit.* (1969), pp.57-62.

Commenting on the value of educational exhibits (in this case, of the Federal Science Pavilion at the Seattle Worlds Fair), Dr Parr, Director of the American Museum of Natural History, surprisingly suggests that the actual factual input is so slight that the purpose of a museum should be directed towards other goals, and his comments merit careful thought. He says:

> The average effects of a visit to an educational exhibit are as a rule so slight they are near or below the limits of accuracy with which such results can be determined.

> The main contribution may lie not in the communication of information but in the reinforcement of knowledge already obtained beforehand and in the stimulation of interest and motivation.

> With a museum it may be more confusing than enlightening to try to relate the functions of the museum directly to ultimate goals. The purpose of a museum is to serve as a means of progress. We should not be preoccupied with the content of a lesson but primarily concerned with the best uses of a tool of communication[10]

The Museum as a Medium

(1) The stored knowledge of a museum, unlike that of the library, archives or pictorial records, is in the form of solid, tangible objects from which information is obtained by direct, sensory examination. Learning from objects is usually a more efficient process and also a more lasting and elemental one because all the senses may be used — to feel, smell, listen, taste and judge dimensions and weight. Museum objects can also be grouped in ways which annihilate time and space. Things made centuries before can be placed beside things made recently, or groupings of objects from widely separated places of origin can provide comparisons and allow new functions to be discovered.

(2) It is a medium which can be understood without the need of written language. The museum artefact is in reality a social document which can be 'read' by close examination and deduction. It is thus peculiarly suited to children and adults who have not learned to read; to handicapped people whose senses enable them to receive direct impressions about these rare things which have been described to them before only in the symbols of words; to children and adults whose learning difficulties hinge on problems with written language; to people whose first language is other than the one currently used. Even if they may not be able to name the artefacts, they will have been able to build up associations in their minds.

(3) It is a medium for direct, personal discovery, available to people of all ages and mental abilities. The value of this must be emphasized. It is the perfect

10. Albert Eide Parr, 'Museums and Realities of Human Existence', in *Museum News*, Washington, DC, Vol. 45, No. 4 (December 1966), pp.24-9.

'It is a medium for direct, personal discovery.' Auckland War Memorial Museum *(Photo: John Buckland).*

open-ended situation for discovery, and teaching strategies with museum objects seek ways by which children can be helped to make their own discoveries. If they can do so, the great advantage of the museum artefact is clear, because it is always there, unchanged, and further direct examination is possible. The skilful teacher can show children that in this situation they can make their own deductions and interpretations in exactly the same way as adults do. The joy of making one's own discoveries is quite different from the tedium of passively absorbing other people's learning and opinions. Demonstrating this to children, while at the same time providing the means of continuing such discoveries, can provide a positive base for new attitudes to learning.

(4) It is a medium capable of arousing our emotions; a process of education which encompasses both the emotions and the intellect in a manner which is the unique advantage of the museum as an educational tool. So intense is this communication that ethical responsibility in its use must be a primary concern of the museum worker. This is because museum collections are not everyday objects but are things of special significance. Because of these qualities and their relationship to wider issues they have been selected for conservation, a skilled and costly process to ensure their continued existence. Even without understanding them, looking at such powerful things often arouses feelings which spill impulsively into active, physical dramatizations.

Two young girls observed recently in the Auckland War Memorial Museum during a lunch break provided an amusing and touching example of this spontaneity. Away from their class and presumably thinking themselves unobserved, they came upon two carved support posts from Maori meeting houses and stopped to gaze at the basal carvings of human figures. Each child, facing a different pole sank to the ground, raised her arms above her head and began salaaming to the floor, saluting the carvings a number of times. Then, laughing, they jumped up and ran away. Similar expressions of spontaneous feeling have been described in the absorbing reports of the Anacostia Neighbourhood Museum set up by the Smithsonian Institution in a socially deprived area with a predominantly Negro population. Viewing materials from Ancient Egypt led to some days of dramatizations and physical expressions before questions began to be asked and investigations began. The study ultimately found expression in a dramatic performance based on the life of those times.[11]

11.   Brief descriptions of the Anacostia experiments may be found in Dillon Ripley, *The Sacred Grove*, *op. cit.*, pp. 105-10, and John Kinard (Director of the Smithsonian Institution's Anacostia Neighbourhood Museum in Washington, DC), *Intermediaries between the Museum and the Community*: Papers from the Ninth Conference of ICOM, *op. cit.*, pp. 151-6.

A particularly strong reaction may occur when one already knows something about events associated with a particular artefact. Where one's imagination has been engaged, being able to handle or merely to touch an authentic object from an area in which one is especially interested can be an experience of great emotional intensity, both to children and adults. There is much we do not know about the effect of objects on man, although we see the force of some encounters in the veneration of religious relics and in the total absorption of some collectors. Few museum objects may be of venerable religious quality, but without question many are able to stir emotions by their qualities and because of the issues to which they relate.

The challenge facing museum educators is how to show these relationships, and, in doing so, to excite what we call the 'sense of wonder' in the child. The museum has been described as the most stimulating medium with which to educate but also the most difficult to use, mainly because each of its artefacts has been removed from the setting in which it originated and which helped to give it meaning. Further, the range of artefacts related to each subject area is almost always incomplete. Objects are bulky to store and items for preservation have to be selected from a wide range, narrowed down to those of greatest significance. From the culture of a whole nation we may have only a dozen items, and full sequences in any museum are rare.

The problem is to know where or how to begin. The use of simplified dramatic settings, mime and role playing for young children supplies some of the necessary background without the need for long verbal or written descriptions. During such activities, good replica material is quite adequate; valuable and fragile materials need not be endangered. With older children, a challenging approach which relates to their personal interests is needed, as is indicated in the following description:

> When, however, the introduction (of a talk or lecture) is carefully related to the needs of a particular group and is aimed at stimulating and encouraging their involvement and participation, it can be of great value. This is the way in which one education officer introduced his subject to a group of bored school leavers who were studying the Victorian period. He was brief and to the point: 'If you had been pregnant a hundred years ago, you would have made baby clothes like these. And if, a few months later, you were in a difficult labour, these are the instruments the doctor would have used to effect the birth — without an anaesthetic.' This startled them. They approached the exhibits that had been specially prepared for them with awe. The education officer stood by, as did their teacher, both waiting for the time when they might be needed to listen, or to answer questions. Before long, the teacher was laughing at the girls' surprise about the length of the baby garments, while the education officer was discussing child mortality and giving further information about the instruments used by the surgeons and doctors.[12]

12. *Pterodactyls and Old Lace:* Museums in Education, *op.cit.,* pp. 26, 27. Further interesting examples are also given in this book.

Mime and role play supply some of the necessary background in a study of Maori tattoo
(Photo: John Buckland).

Such emotional responses are not everyday experiences, but the fact that they can and do occur must constantly be kept in mind because of the powerful influence they can exert in determining patterns of thought. Close to our emotions lies our sense of values, and the implications of this in the education of young people cannot be ignored, and indeed the consequences of doing so occur in warnings in the writings of a number of people today. If through these experiences we enable young people to feel a sense of excitement and joy in learning and if at the same time we introduce them to a place where the possibility of this is unlimited, we may give them a new impetus. If we can give them a sense of kinship with people of other races and cultures by providing insight into their lives and achievements, we can set a better basis for human understanding. If these experiences are linked through material objects whose existence depends on special protection and care, and, not least, if the experiences have been exciting and personal, we have an opportunity to establish greater respect and appreciation of public material assets and property. These objectives are well summarized by A.E. Parr when he writes:

> Because the teachings of a museum are presented not primarily in the abstract symbols of language that are the main tools of the classroom, but by demonstrations of the actual or reconstructed evidence from which our knowledge of nature is obtained, museum exhibits also afford an opportunity for the child to make its first acquaintance with the deductive method of science from the moment the first seeds of scientific curiosity are planted in the mind.[13] . . . *The development of proper habits of thought and feelings is the least postponable aspect of education.* The negative open-mindedness of emptiness must be converted into reasoned objectivity; feelings must be given adequate scope, and orientation and prejudices must be balanced by counter-prejudices before the pattern hardens. The importance of museum services for children springs from the great roles they can, and often do play, among the early influences that largely determine our responses to all later education and training and to life itself.[14] (Italics mine)

Although such outcomes may be expected from successful visits, some visits may prove disappointing and, when these occur, attitudes are likely to be polarized, with the result that children may not wish to return to the museum. Ian Findlay goes as far as to suggest that in Great Britain this negative attitude has led to contempt and even to vandalism. He states:

> Perhaps what the 'normal' child is deprived of is a sense of wonder. Its television screens ensure that nothing is unfamiliar to it, and familiarity without real knowledge breeds contempt. The contempt may turn out to be one of the breeders of vandalism and it is significant that vandalism by young people in museums has increased enormously since the war.[15]

As far as can be seen from publications up to the present time, the chances of having unsatisfactory visits to museums for school classes increase for a number of reasons:

(1) If the visit seems to the child to be similar to school experiences.

(2) If the child has no opportunity to make his own discovery.

(3) If the child has no opportunity to ask his own questions at the appropriate time.

13. 'Why Children's Museums?' in *Curator*, New York, NY, Vol. 3, No. 3 (1960), p. 234.
14. *Ibid.*, p. 232.
15. Ian Findlay, *Priceless Heritage: the Future of Museums* (London: Faber and Faber, 1977), p. 94.

'Experiences linked through objects whose existence depends on special protection and care'
(Photo: National Museum).

(4) If he is unable to express his feelings and the emotions roused by the encounter adequately.

(5) If he fails to grasp the significance of what is being shown to him because of inadequate background knowledge. This, the hardest to accomplish for the museum teacher, is the most crucial.

Thus we see that the aim of museums is to introduce children from all sections of the community to the use and enjoyment of them on a basis which could become permanent. As museums are places which ultimately are visited and used only on a voluntary basis, these objectives will probably not be realized unless the first visits of the child are pleasurable.

In New Zealand the museum visit undertaken by school classes is at present regarded as the first and best strategy to teach children the skills needed to look at and appreciate museum objects, particularly when groups are small and discussion by the children is encouraged. The second strategy, to use museums for personal encounters, could be facilitated by provision for leisure and voluntary activities. As discussed elsewhere, encounters with objects of special interest are more likely to occur when personal initiatives are followed and the powerful responses which contact with these artefacts may bring are completely private.

Both strategies could be facilitated by a structured approach.

(1) *The group or class visit* where children handle, discuss, examine and dramatize with objects.

(2) *Visits with increasing emphasis on personal investigation.* This would continue to use the group unit; the small group to allow the children to hold discussions, and the larger group to provide an outlet for the expression of the emotions these objects produce. Personal investigation should have increasing emphasis at the intermediate and secondary school levels.

(3) *Provision for voluntary, leisure activities for children* who find the museum a place of particular interest. Children's centres could be set up and staffed in the larger museums, providing for the leisure interests of both young and adolescent children. Such centres would then be available, as in museums overseas, for use in the evenings by adult groups. Responsibility for these would lie with the museum education department. Education officers could contribute towards staffing out of school hours as part of their duties, as also could all museum staff.

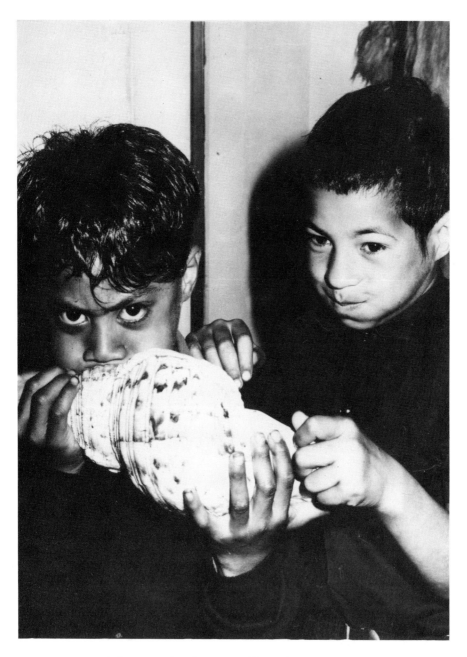

'...to feel a sense of excitement and joy in learning' (Photo: John Buckland).

4 Museums, Schools and the Class Teacher

The use of museums by schools is entirely optional and requires initiative on the part of each class teacher who wishes to use them. Not all museums have special services and those that do must see that in their district as many school principals and teachers as possible are fully informed about them. Staff changes and turnover require regular and efficient communication.

How Schools Find out about Museum Services

All museum education services send out circulars to each school principal in its education board area annually, either for display, such as the posters from Manawatu Museum which they print on their own presses, or notices and programmes to file in the principal's office or in the staffroom. Increasingly these are descriptions of the range of materials in the museum collections rather than titles of general lesson topics, except for temporary teaching exhibitions. The method usually works well, but the human element has to be taken into account. Most education officers keep records of their contacts with each school so that, when a particular school does not use their resources for some time, they find ways of visiting it. Several ring and offer to come to a staff meeting after school; or call in with a museum loan case and chat to the principal; or find someone on the staff whom they can inform. Some spend several weeks at the beginning of each year touring schools in selected areas, talking to the staffs, and displaying museum cases. They may also send out circulars and newsletters each term. As a result, communication between museums and schools appears to be satisfactory.

Museum advisory committees help to inform as well as assist in planning. Each education officer works directly under a district senior inspector, some of whom have set up these informal committees, chaired by him or his representative. These committees usually include the director of the museum, members of the Principal's Association, the NZEI, teachers college staff and the normal school, science and art and craft advisers and the education officer. In this way, informed contacts with all these bodies are provided. Similar advisory committees in Great Britain are described by Victoria Airey.[1]

In-service courses for teachers and principals are being held more frequently. Museums usually invite a representative from each school, although some courses are not aimed initially at representative attendance. The most successful are those where teachers or principals engage actively in discovery or creative activities in the same manner as the children do, and these are replacing those based on descriptions of services for which demand is waning. Courses on Maori tools, for example, provide an opportunity for teachers to examine and learn how to use them as well as make their own replicas. In this way, while teaching a skill, museums may increase their own supply of handling material. Personal experience is the best way to appreciate the quality of a museum visit. The departing school principal with a Maori flute he has made using only primitive stone tools, has a new and deeper concept of the value of this type of experience. Courses such as 'Local Maori Legends of the Manawatu' have been flooded with applications for attendance. They usually occur one evening a week for a month or six weeks, occasionally in blocked time during the school term. Undoubtedly this type of course, aimed at personal involvement, meets the needs of the teachers in a new way. As fewer new teachers receive museum training at teachers college, in-service courses are of increasing importance.

Bookings for visits are made by telephone or by mail. Mailed bookings involve the use of forms in which each school lists its requirements at the beginning of the school term, enabling a number of reservations to be made at one time. Written confirmation in the form of a master copy for the principal and individual memos for the class teachers confirms the dates. This is useful for museum services who have no aide to answer the telephone, although all education officers list times before and after school and during lunch hour when they can be contacted. Telephone bookings give an opportunity for discussion regarding suitable timing and the emphasis the class teacher wishes the lesson to have. Written confirmation then follows. The teacher is invited to visit, if unfamiliar with the museum, for a preliminary look at the material. Preparatory notes may also be sent out to the school, or references given to such material on the museum file at the school. Most museums require from one week to one month's notice of an intended visit, and most schools have to wait for an appointment. As the timetable for the term is filled, late applicants may have a long wait, or may not be able to

1. *Museums and Children:* Monographs on Education, *op.cit.,* p.158.

receive an appointment. The unsatisfied demand has unfortunately not been recorded in sufficient detail to support requests for additional staffing. Materials to assist with follow-up work are issued after the visit.

Role of the Class Teacher

Formerly this was a passive one, the visit being taken over entirely by education staff and students on arrival. The teacher, free to observe all groups, usually took notes. The move to bring teachers into the planning, to structure the presentation of the material with the emphasis requested by the teacher, is to be commended. The visit to the museum is only part of a study in the classroom, and provision of information about museum collections, from which the teacher can plan, is a positive move. Therefore, preparation beforehand and follow-up work later is essential if full advantage is to be taken of the visit.

In the larger museums, teachers are being brought in more to participate in the gallery teaching, a move which is to be regretted. Those who are familiar with the materials, particularly those with museum teaching experience, usually prefer to conduct their own classes. The galleries are open to all and any teacher may reserve specified exhibits for his or her class to study. The insecure teacher has to forgo the chance to see an expert at work and may not be aware of the particular problems which teaching with museum objects presents. Teachers are more likely to use collections in ways already familiar to the children, and all museum professionals emphasize that a museum visit must be quite different from a classroom situation. While directed to study, it should also be aimed at providing an interesting experience in its own right.

Some teachers understand this already and make enlightened experiments of their own, but this is unusual. The education officer who has both teaching and museum experience ought to be able to enrich the teacher's programme with an appropriate and stimulating contribution. Children do not automatically become involved with exhibits just because they are handling them. They have to be encouraged to investigate, to find out, to compare weight and texture. They have to learn how to acquire greater insight and more acute perception of qualities inherent in the object, and seeing a specialist look at, handle, examine and assess such objects leads to awareness of this kind.

The Single Visit

Many school classes, particularly when visiting other towns, undertake single visits which if planned can be valuable and open wider ranges of museums.

The quality of some of our small local museums is very high, providing opportunities to see unique collections related to local industries or local history. One problem is that teachers may lack background knowledge of these places. As the sum of our museum resources is one of our great national assets, either the Art Galleries and Museums Association of New Zealand (AGMANZ) or the Department of Education should examine ways in which staffs of the small museums, operating on tiny budgets and dependent on volunteer help can provide such information to enable better preparation to be made beforehand. They should also be helped to handle such visits.

The unplanned, single visit is a headache to all museums, many of whom would like to see it banned, but, as their galleries are public institutions, this is not possible unless damage occurs. There often seems little purpose in such visits except to provide an outing and to see something which is regarded as entertaining and recreative, even if it is only peripherally related to what the children are doing. A general visit can trigger off an unrecognized interest but at best this is likely to affect only a minority of children and is more likely to turn merely into a diversion. Such unplanned visits should be discouraged.

The Extended Visit

As mentioned in Chapter 1, most class visits have been of 1-2 hours duration, but the current trend is to expand to half or whole day visits or even as long as a week. The longer period of time has many advantages, but its drawback is that it restricts the facilities to a smaller number of classes. Only Otago Museum has facilities extensive enough to permit short and long visits concurrently. Evaluation of these is needed. Fewer but more satisfying visits could well be better for whole classes, with additional supplementary visits of small groups in the care of a parent if more information is required.

It is likely that the extended visit may be the key to better use of museums for children, with the opportunities this provides to study or engage in creative work in depth. Rising transport costs which are likely to limit visits may be justified by visits of longer duration.

Visits for Personal Study Related to School Programmes

As the museum is established essentially as a research institution and exists to provide both leisure entertainment and opportunities for learning on an individual basis, teaching the child from an early age to use these resources himself is desirable. Experiments at the National Museum some years ago were directed at this personal level with primary school children from S3 upwards. It was suggested to the class teacher that after the visit of the whole class, selected children might return in school time in the care of a parent for further study in their own areas of interest. The education officer, notified of the visit, could be consulted by the children. These visits appeared to achieve for these children the quiet time needed for personal perusal and thought. Some occasions developed into intensive learning situations calling for expertise and information not only from the education officer but also from the appropriate museum expert. They also provided a quiet opportunity to look at other museum exhibits without the distraction of a larger group, and appeared suitable for the levels at which they were tried.

Returns of Attendance

All education services supply attendance figures annually both to the museum director and to the district senior inspector, but the method by which they are prepared has not been standardized. Some returns are related to visits which may be of short or long duration; others adjust to one-hour units, a method used initially by Auckland War Memorial Museum whose records since 1941 are the most complete (see Table A2). In this museum, a visit of half-an-hour for 40 children would be registered as 20 units, while 40 children on a longer visit might count as 40 x 4 hours= 1,600 units. All four main museums now use the one-hour unit and all newer museum services might consider adopting this system to facilitate comparisons, for example, when new staffing is being considered. Figures based on different units fail to reveal the true picture, and, for this reason, tables of attendance at the 13 currently operating centres have not been given.

A standard method of recording attendances would be useful, and so would a record showing details of class levels and the areas of the museum which are being used.

Attendance figures have always been an issue. All museums except the National Museum have to find their operating funds, mainly from local bodies. Returns relating to children's services have been used extensively in preparing cases to put before them for financial support, and there has been pressure on some education officers to produce figures showing satisfactory attendances, preferably with a steady annual increase. Possibly because of this as well as their reluctance to use a numerical yardstick against which to evaluate their work, little detail has been kept. Few analyse the age or class level of the children or record the subject areas for which demand has been highest, although Figures A1 to A3, and Table A5, drawn up by W.A.K. Berry at the Auckland War Memorial Museum, show the usefulness of such analysis. Fluctuations caused by many extraneous factors, such as transport difficulties, petrol restrictions, polio epidemics, staffing changes, alterations to buildings, the opening of new premises and stimulating temporary exhibitions have been evened out by expressing annual totals from the first four centres (Table A1) as a percentage of the total school rolls for the country taken from the E-1 Report of the Department of Education. These indicate that growth has been in keeping with the natural increase. Unfortunately records of the unsatisfied demand for bookings have not been recorded consistently enough to allow analysis.

Their first glimpse inside an old slab hut (Photo: Gisbourne Herald).

Age Levels of Different Classes

Pre-school groups are visiting museums more frequently and the interest level is high. It is interesting to look through old annual reports and to see how education officers who initially set limits from about S3 up gradually relaxed this stance and recorded with enthusiasm the response of younger children. It is appropriate to their stage of learning which does not yet involve the use of written language. Details related to the number of children making such visits would be useful.

Intermediate schools use museums more than do post-primary schools, and less than *primary schools,* as shown in Tables A3, A4. Records from the Auckland War Memorial Museum (Tables A2, A3) provide data from which it has been possible to express their attendances as a percentage of the total national rolls of primary, intermediate and post-primary schools taken from E-1 Report of the Department of Education. From this we see that in 1977 8.19 percent of national totals of primary schools made visits to this museum compared with 6.06 percent of intermediate rolls and 2.71 percent of post-primary rolls. A voluntary activity at intermediate level provides museum electives for nearby schools in some areas. These are among the few voluntary services available for children and they meet the needs of children in another way.

Secondary schools use museums far less than is desirable and this applies to other countries as well as to New Zealand. At the Auckland War Memorial Museum (Table A3) attendance figures for 1960-77, expressed as a percentage of the national rolls, ranged from 8.19 to 12.36 percent for primary schools; 4.01 to 11.71 percent for intermediate schools, and 1.31 to 3.94 percent for post-primary school rolls. In Canterbury (Table A4) there were attendances of 5.88 to 7.31 percent for primary and 0.47 to 2.78 percent for post-primary rolls. The National Museum records 3 post-primary visits compared with 307 primary classes in 1968, 27 post-primary to 620 primary in 1973, and 37 post-primary to 607 primary in 1978. The demand comes mainly from classes of low academic performance. This appears to be a world trend, despite the recommendations of Unesco and national educational bodies. As Ian Findlay says:

> The most formidable part of the problem of how to draw schools and museums closer is to discover how museums can help in secondary education. It is doubtful if any serious progress has been made in studies to this end, either in this country or in any in the Western world, including America, in the last decade or two.[2]

At the root of the problem lies the timetable structure of the secondary schools where pupils change from one teacher to another for different sub-

---

2. Ian Findlay, *Priceless Heritage: The Future of Museums* (London: Faber and Faber, 1977), p. 97

jects. The demands of the syllabus, particularly at senior levels, also require time to be used intensively to cover examination requirements. To compensate for travelling time, a teaching situation of high quality is called for. These children, at an emotional and vulnerable age, need challenging experiences in learning, with greater attention paid to working purposefully in a more sustained way. Some smaller museums provide graduate scientific staff to teach at this level where the education officer is not scientifically trained, but generally they offer lectures on currently exhibited collections. Children are given few or no opportunities to use museum resources actively for their own studies.

Another factor might be that the policy of the education officers is directed by the district senior inspectors, which would tend to direct services and new developments towards the primary school system. Some direct, official linkage between the education officers and the post-primary inspectorate is desirable if mutually fruitful initiatives are to be discussed and tried out.

It would be possible to second people engaged in curriculum development as well as staff from the secondary teachers colleges to examine and select resources suitable for these age levels. As the colleges in both Christchurch and Auckland are close to museums with extensive collections and resources, secondary school student teachers could be posted there for blocked periods of teaching practice. Some compelling interviews on the use of the museum for training were held with teachers who had had a museum section during their one year of training at a secondary teachers college. The extent to which the Auckland teachers colleges have used the Auckland War Memorial Museum is shown in Table A6.

If adequately prepared, secondary school children can work independently on materials which provide immediate encounters with authenticity, are conducive to independent thinking and can bring respect for other people and for the material objects which reveal them to us. These values are of direct importance to a number of the social problems which present-day social adolescent behaviour highlights, and those responsible for education at this level might give careful consideration to the provision of adequately structured museum experiences not only to meet the needs of low-stream levels, but also those of high intellect whose abilities need challenging and stimulating tasks.

A successful experiment with secondary school pupils at the Geological and Mining Museum, The Rocks, Sydney has been developed in the past two years by its education officer, Brian Garner. This museum is often visited by secondary school classes for whose visits a lecture, a film and a guided tour in the galleries were customary. The time spent in these activities has now been reduced and a room provided with tables for group work with directions and implements for the students to investigate mineral specimens. Study time has increased with greater commitment and satisfaction on the part of the students.

Services Provided outside the Museum

1. *An identification service of plants, insects, minerals,* and so on, is provided with help from professional museum staff.

2. *Special displays in schools* mounted in the foyer or the library. Difficulties stem from the limited staffing available to prepare and service the displays as well as the shortage of suitable materials. Such displays are worth developing where circumstances are favourable.

3. *Visits to special institutions, for example, children's hospital wards, borstals and prisons, institutions for the handicapped.* The success of trial visits clearly indicate the need for such services. In Wellington and Auckland most prison work, particularly with Maori inmates, has been done by professional museum staff. They have taken the inmates artefacts relating to their history and have started carving classes with them in Auckland. Ways of continuing and extending this service might be considered. Children in hospital benefit greatly from handling material and from the stimulus of the visit. In the smaller centres where the education officers often know the children personally, more pleasure is added to the visit. Hospital staff are in favour of the development.

4. *Extension of work outside museum walls.* Museum work should relate not only to the schools but also to the community. Involvement in wider community educational programmes, such as WEA, university extension courses, teachers and PTA meetings, and so on, needs to be regarded as a normal part of the work of a museum education officer. The article, 'Museums and Adult Education' by Alan M. Eyles, Assistant Education Officer, Canterbury Museum, surveys the work done in Canterbury Museum through the WEA, and indicates the aspects of these classes which have been the most successful.[3] Use of news media by earlier education officers has lapsed as the gap between them and museum staffs has widened. Both museum staff and education officers should be actively involved, as this serves the vital function of introducing museum artefacts to the public, drawing them into the museum for the purpose of viewing them.

AGMANZ News is readily available for the publication of specialist papers,

3. *WEA Review*, October 1970, pp.124-6.

and responsibility to provide this material lies with the education officers. Publication of articles describing recent experimental educational work by museum staffs is very useful. [4,5]

5. *Visits to the schools.* Some education officers take selected handling material and teach in the schools. This is a service which schools would like to see developed, and about which museums have reservations, as they feel this might come between the children and their chance to visit a museum. But there is a number of arguments in its favour:

(1) Such a visit may arouse curiosity sufficiently to bring children into the museum on their own.
(2) It may provide the element appropriate to the classroom without endangering the museum concept of discovery within the gallery.
(3) It would reduce the cost of transporting children to the museum.
(4) It could reach a larger number of children, particularly when combined with special displays.

There are several purposes for which education officers in general may undertake visits to schools:

(1) To take lessons preparatory to a museum visit.
(2) To arouse interest in visiting the museum.
(3) As an Outreach programme for distant schools unable to visit museums, often using special displays.
(4) To teach handicapped children.
(5) To participate in follow-up activities.

In New Zealand, the visit to arouse interest in the museum may take place at the beginning of the school year. In the lull before class visits begin, education officers call at schools which they have noted do not use their services, or follow a circuit outside their immediate area. Teaching of preparatory lessons is usually restricted by the demands on staffing and is seldom possible. Instead, information, illustrations, references, and so on, are usually sent to the class teacher.

The Outreach-type programme has not been developed in New Zealand but is an important part of the work of education officers in Australia. Schools or community centres are used as venues to set up exhibitions, to which visits are

4. Ken Gorbey, 'IYC at WAM — Children as Research Assistants', in *AGMANZ News*, Auckland, Vol. 10, No. 2 (May 1979), pp.7, 8.
5. David Butts, 'Education in the Round — Cooperative Planning', in *AGMANZ News*, Auckland, Vol. 11, No. 3 (August 1980), pp.2, 3.

arranged for a wide range of age levels, so that whole schools may participate in a museum-inspired study.

The Australian Museum, Sydney, uses two railway carriages equipped with audio-visual aids and special exhibitions. These carriages, shunted to local sidings, are staffed by two education officers who teach school classes during the day and community groups and individual visitors in the evenings and at weekends. This museum also uses a specially equipped van to visit institutions for the handicapped.

The recent drop in attendances of school classes here, noted by many museums (see Tables A1, A2) has been attributed to the escalating costs of transport and this Outreach-type programme might well be considered as an alternative to the museum visit. Carefully evaluated trials in this area would be very useful.

Varying reasons for extension services are given in *Museums and Children*,[6] which summarizes education services in 14 countries. Maureen Gee[7] describes visits in Canada to overcome the problems of lack of space in the museum as well as the problems of preparation before a museum visit. In the USA, Bonnie Pitman-Gelles[8] describes classroom presentations of 20 minutes to 2 hours duration by staff and volunteers, within an hour's driving distance from the museum. In the United Kingdom, according to Victoria Airey,[9] there is a 'policy of going out to (rural) schools to keep in touch, to give talks, take teaching collections to handle in the classroom, observe the use of loan materials and take part in follow-up activities'. She feels that while it is helpful in reducing transport costs for rural schools or those in deprived areas of cities, it is not a satisfactory substitute for a visit to the comprehensive collections in the museum.

6. *School loan cases* have been prepared and circulated from the four principal museum centres since 1938. Earliest education officers had to prepare these themselves but, since 1943, or later in most centres, technicians appointed by the Department of Education have prepared and maintained them. The cases are provided by the Department of Education and the contents by the museums.

The National Museum provides a nucleus of these cases for loan from the newer museum education centres of Nelson, Manawatu, Wanganui, Taranaki, Napier, Gisborne and Waikato.

Surprisingly little change has occurred in the design of many cases, and the

6. *Museums and Children:* Monographs on Education, *op.cit.*
7. *Ibid.*, p.70.
8. *Ibid.*, p.176.
9. *Ibid.*, p. 152.

original type, known as the Carnegie case, which is illustrated on pp.29-30 of McQueen's *Education in New Zealand Museums*, is still in use. Other cases contain mounted birds which some museums lend separately, or displays of artefacts and materials related to each museum's collections and strengths, usually mounted behind glass. Beautifully prepared models and dioramas circulate from Auckland and Canterbury. Sets of historical photographs lent from most museums are often used for preparation and for follow-up work in schools. Boxes of handling specimens of shells and rocks are available, but there are surprisingly few resource boxes of handling artefacts, despite the emphasis placed on handling materials in the galleries. Suggestions to develop museums as centres for different types of teaching aids have been raised periodically, but decisions have consistently affirmed that loan materials should be related only to collections which museums possess.

An innovative type of display case, hinged to fold in three sections, has been developed at the National Museum. Unlike the smaller cases which only 2 or 3 children can use at a time, these are suitable for larger groups and for display in a classroom, library or school foyer. The artefacts or excellent replicas are loose and usually can be removed for handling. Their size increases the cost of transport but they have significant advantages, and experiments in this area are needed.

Resource kits of slides, cassette tapes, illustrations, replica handling materials and information on a particular topic are in contrast to the presentation, behind glass, of materials related to one theme. Some resource kits, for example, 18 at Canterbury Museum prepared by the Environmental Resources In-Service Training Course, are available, but more are needed.

Loans are made directly to teachers who can call after school to collect and return them. In country areas, a group of schools usually select a range of cases which they will share for a term. These are available from a local school, or similar centre, such as a small museum. Canterbury has a direct service to all schools within the board area, and cases are sent for a period of three weeks. Accompanying notes may be retained by the teacher. The question of direct or indirect circulation hinges on finance. Direct service in Canterbury provides the material when the teacher wants it, which means its value is greatly enhanced, but it is more expensive. It is much less useful to get a case for general interest only, but this method is cheaper and is used by all other centres. The dilemma has not been satisfactorily resolved over the 40-year period of operation, and changes in methods of circulation centre on these two variables.

Evaluation of loan services is urgently needed as are experiments to try out new methods of using and distributing these materials. Each of the four centres, where travelling materials are prepared, should undertake an experimental programme which could include:

(1) New types of circulating loan cases.

(2) Displays mounted in school libraries or foyers.

(3) Mobile services for special institutions, for example, hospitals, prisons, senior citizen centres and homes, institutions for the physically and mentally handicapped.

(4) Provision of temporary displays for use in museums where there is only one education officer. Such museums usually have a classroom or part of a gallery for temporary exhibitions. Temporary displays would widen the repertoire of these museums. Each could be mounted at a museum for a school term, moving to the next museum during the school holidays. It would also be useful to use one centre to produce high quality replica artefacts, or to arrange exchanges of these between museums.

A typical display from the early 1940s, on New Zealand moths, in a 1938 Carnegie-type case. Many of these cases are still in circulation (Photo: National Museum).

'Museum education staff provide an independent evaluation of the quality of teaching of each student' (Photo: John Buckland).

5   The Education Officer

As we have seen, the education officers who are trained teachers appointed permanently to the museums are the principal agents working with school classes here. Attached administratively to local schools, they are not members of the museum staffs. They do little work with leisure activities or with individual children, concentrating instead on visits to the museum of classes from pre-school to secondary level, with some teachers college groups, but principally they are concerned with primary school children. Classrooms are available in some museums which most use for informal activities, despite the presence of school desks and tables. They visit schools at times with teaching materials, but work mainly in the museum galleries. They operate a loan service of cases and illustrative materials after school hours and within the geographic area of each museum, using public transport. They work closely with museum staffs to which they do not belong, have rare professional contacts with each other, and have no career structure. A number has stayed for extended periods, two for about 30 years each. Long periods of service have also been built up by prolonged tenure of assistant positions, followed by appointment to the senior position. The total number of education officers throughout the country at present is 20, comprising 4 senior education officers, 12 assistants or education officers working on their own, and 4 part-time education officers. There are 4 art technicians who are not teachers.

Appointment of Education Officers

Unlike the situation in most other countries on which there is published information, in New Zealand, the Department of Education appoints and employs most museum education staff; only two are known at present to be employed by other agencies. In Britain various methods of appointment, outlined in *Museums in Education:* Education Survey, No. 12,[1] include educa-

1. *Museums in Education:* Education Survey, No. 12, *op.cit.*, p.4

tion officers in school employ who are seconded to museums; some in museum employ but salaried by the education authorities; some in situations salaried by a combination of museums and education authorities. In most national museums they are the direct employees of the museum, deeply involved in the museum's work with the public at all age levels — with children and adults, formal and informal visits, enquiries, loan collections and publications.

In Australia there are similar wide variations in appointments which the Museums Education Association of Australia is at present surveying. Secondment from the teaching service is common. Positions are advertised, but tenure for only one or two years may be mandatory. Reappointment is rare, and generally refused. While some continue to work school hours and observe school holidays, others are paid an extra standard allowance to work the hours and take holidays appropriate to people in administrative positions. Few museums have permanently appointed education officers on their staffs, but those that do, principally national museums, have an opportunity to develop more structured and longer evaluated activities.

Almost all education officers in these countries are both university graduates and trained, certificated teachers who generally have had several years of teaching experience beforehand in schools. A minority of New Zealand education officers are graduates but all are trained teachers, as are, incidentally, a number of museum directors.

Method of Appointment

Vacancies are advertised in the official *Education Gazette* and applicants are screened, interviewed and appointed by a legally constituted committee, which since 1956 has not included the director of the museum concerned. The qualities sought are determined by a committee which, according to Education (Assessment, Classification and Appointment) Regulation SR 1976/287, comprises the district senior inspector, the chairman of the education board and a representative of the New Zealand Educational Institute. When these regulations were first framed in 1956, aiming at limiting the size of the appointments committee, the museum situation was probably overlooked. Before this, between 1941-56, the director of the museum concerned participated in the selection process, identifying areas of interest appropriate to that museum and helping to choose people with qualifications appropriate to their collections and personalities compatible with those of the museum staffs. It is astonishing that so many years have elapsed since this legislation was passed without some discussion on this question taking place between the education authorities and AGMANZ.

The directors have chafed at their exclusion, unaware of this legislation. Specific departures exist for normal schools and integrated private schools when appropriate, and AGMANZ could make representation for similar departures for museum education appointments, although this would still not confer voting rights on the directors. There are therefore grounds for a review of this situation. Museum directors are intimately concerned with education policy in their museums and closely involved with its day-to-day implementation. It is of vital concern that the education officers should work harmoniously with their staffs.

Control

Since 1966 the work of the education officers has been directed by the district senior inspector (DSI) or his representative who may choose to set up an advisory committee, as described in Chapter 4, with the dual function of guiding museum services on school needs and keeping schools informed about museum services. This committee, chaired by the DSI, usually includes the director of the museum, who thus has an opportunity to influence developing policy. Otherwise, the only control the director can officially exert is the power of veto to prohibit what is considered an undesirable use of artefacts or unsuitable activities within the museum galleries. Undoubtedly the present administrative procedures have several disadvantages.

Funding

The division of responsibility for providing services and operating costs, as mentioned in Chapter 2, was clearly defined between both parties in 1941. These earlier agreements have been lost sight of and wrangles have occurred subsequently as services spread to other museums. New national guidelines, available to both parties, should be drawn up in discussion between museums and the Department of Education. Funding, which is currently at the discretion of each education board, is erratic and unduly restrictive for some museum services. Some operate on funding as low as $30-34[2] annually while in an adjacent education board area the allocation for similar staffing may be $200. There appears to be no policy regarding provision of special equipment, such as audio-visual aids, for the use of newly appointed education officers.

A review of the equipment and facilities used by the education officers was

2. Initial allocation for Wanganui Public Museum for 1978.

prepared by John Christie, Education Officer, National Museum, in 1973.[3] As this was found to vary widely he suggested that a list of basic equipment similar to that of Group 2 schools would be useful. In addition, he suggested that the grants allocated to the education boards by the Director General of Education for supplying and maintaining educational services in museums should be available in full to the museum officers. If notified of the total grant, financial planning and budgeting could be undertaken.

Administration by the Department of Education

When only four centres were operating, responsibility was at Departmental level through the Supervisor of Visual Aids, W.B. Harris, who travelled annually to each centre and attended the biennial conference of AGMANZ. The Director of Education at that time was Dr C.E. Beeby, formerly Director, NZCER, during the three-year period when this council administered the Carnegie grant and monitored these experiments. Guidelines for funding and professional development had been clearly defined.

Regional control has largely removed responsibility from the Department of Education, but better coordination where it could assist the DSIs is urgently needed at this level. A senior departmental officer, familiar with museums and their needs, with status and continued responsibilities similar to the officer concerned with museums and art galleries in the Department of Internal Affairs, could coordinate policy and act both as a reference for the various regions and as a contact with professional museum organizations.

In 1969 and 1975, surveys containing perceptive and useful recommendations were prepared on museum education services. These have been the work of temporarily seconded officers whose transfer before recommendations could be actioned has caused disappointment.

Representation at Museum Conferences

The Department of Education should be represented once more, as is the Department of Internal Affairs, at AGMANZ conferences, enabling it to keep in touch with, and assess, current developments. The representative of the Department of Internal Affairs is a member of AGMANZ Council and such representation should be extended to the Department of Education.

Education Department officers from several states in Australia are represented at conferences of the Museums Education Association of Australia.

3. J.A. Christie, 'Report upon Equipment for Museum Education Services', National Museum, February 1973 (mimeo).

Career Opportunities

There is no career structure for museum education officers, although the positions are permanent. Since 1941, when the Department of Education took over responsibility for the museum education services, there has been a conflict between it and the education officers over salaries and length of tenure. The education authorities, quoting as examples the professional distinction of the careers of the four education officers involved in the three-year experimental period, have constantly hoped for more movement of such officers through the museum services, returning to schools as resource people. The salary range of education officers has been limited to encourage return to schools, but this has not had the desired effect. During the past 35 years the education officers have unsuccessfully appealed against these limitations on a number of occasions, both directly to the Department of Education as well as through NZEI. During this time their salary relativities have been progressively downgraded compared with those of school positions. Directors of museums also wish to see more movement, as well as younger people in these positions, and 10 years was suggested as the maximum length of tenure. The limited tenure in Australia, where one or two years is customary, indicates a similar policy. Limited tenure is also supported by many education officers.

In his annual report for 1979, the Senior Education Officer of the Auckland War Memorial Museum, W.A.K. Berry, who had been in this position for seven years stated:

> I am now of the opinion that School Service appointments to museums should be of limited tenure, thus ensuring a two-way flow of ideas from and to the mainstream of teaching with its ever changing emphasis. In addition, this would ensure a supply to the schools of a group of teachers experienced and enlightened in the value of museums as teaching resources. Some form of secondment from schools for a year may achieve both these goals while at the same time increasing the entitlement of School Service staff.

The first advertisements for these positions in 1937 were for a limited tenure of three years, yet they attracted numerous applicants from whom four highly qualified men were selected. Of these only one, R.A. Scobie, Education Officer at Auckland Museum, occupied the position for many years when the positions were made permanent, combining it with work as a lecturer in anthropology at Auckland University. D.W. McKenzie, Education Officer at the Dominion (now National) Museum, ended his career as Associate Professor of Geography at Victoria University of Wellington; George Guy, Education Officer, Canterbury Museum, became Principal, Canterbury Teachers College; Gordon Anderson, Education Officer, Otago Museum, became Senior Inspector of Secondary Schools, South Auckland district.

Between 1941-79, including present incumbents, there have been 3 senior education officers in Auckland, 6 in Wellington, 5 in Christchurch and 3 in Dunedin. Apart from war-time caretaker appointments, only two women have been appointed to these senior positions, both at the National Museum. Of the 13 previous education officers, 4 have retired from these positions at the end of their careers; R.A. Scobie (Auckland) retired after 34 years, and L. Lockerbie (Otago) after 29 years.

Salary and status structures for museum education officers involve complex and at times conflicting issues because of the special positions they occupy. It is important that they be teachers of superior ability because:

(1) They always teach in public and are therefore under constant observation. It is a position of public relations for the Department of Education and makes a significant contribution to its prestige. Museum classes frequently have a 'tail' of interested adults.

(2) They always teach in front of the class teacher who sees children they know well responding to someone else, thus providing an opportunity to demonstrate good teaching techniques to a wide range of teachers.

(3) They have been deeply involved in the training of student groups from the teachers colleges. As we see from Table A7, between 1959–66, over 400 students annually were given 4 weeks training at 4 centres, a relatively higher ratio of students to associate teacher than occurs elsewhere. In 1978, 120 students had museum training in 6 centres.

It follows that museum education officers should be stimulating and creative teachers and that they should use teaching methods consistent with modern developments.

Museum directors suggest:

(1) Limited tenure. This was unanimous. The maximum figure suggested for education officers was 10 years; for assistant education officers, 2 or 3 years.

(2) Younger people in these positions.

(3) Education officers who are in close touch with the schools and thoroughly conversant with new developments in teaching practice and the curriculum.

(4) Education officers who would be involved in additional leisure time activities with children.

(5) Participation by the director in the selection process for appointments.

Education officers suggest:

(1) Limited tenure, although they approach this with some caution. They

feel they have reduced prospects for advancement after a few years in a museum.

(2) Improved salaries with better status and career prospects.

(3) Realistic advancement opportunities into other areas where their special knowledge would be useful. After a few years in the museum, they have acquired a rich and varied background knowledge but possibly lack the formal qualifications that would indicate this.

Summary of recommendations:

(1) Improved salaries with better status and good career prospects, tied to a defined period of tenure.

(2) Protected re-employment as well as realistic advancement opportunities.

(3) Use of secondment at all levels from assistants to curriculum development personnel.

(4) Compulsory service in schools between the positions of assistant and senior education officer.

(5) Regular review of part-time appointments, preferably by readvertising the positions annually.

(6) Appointment by the Department of Education instead of by education boards.

(7) Recognition of service in museums as of value applicable to some other specialist services, for example, in the teaching of science, social studies, or as museum resource staff in schools.

Personal Qualities of the Museum Educator

The success or failure of museum education programmes stems primarily from the personality of the educator. Speaking on this in relation to the education services in the United Kingdom, T.A. Hume, Director of Liverpool Museums, stated:

> It would be difficult to find any downright bad service in these islands of ours, but it is perhaps beyond question that the most distinguished and often most unorthodox schemes derive much of their exceptional merit from the personality of their creators. Only in such cases does one feel that the full potential of museums is realized.[4]

4. T.A. Hume, 'Museums and Education in the United Kingdom', in *The Role of Museums in Education*, Australian Unesco Seminar (Sydney, 1966).

Similarly, Ian Findlay, former Director of the Royal Scottish Museum, when commenting on the problem of finding suitable people, particularly for teaching secondary school pupils, states:

> Not the least (of the practical difficulties) is the recruitment of the right men and women on the museum side. It is not a matter of transferring teachers to the museum service. If they are to stir the interest of pupils who are there for the negative reason that they are not academically minded, they have to be natural interpreters — people so committed to and excited by their subject, that their enthusiasm is catching. The aim is to put flesh on the bones of history, anthropology, biology and other disciplines, to give such studies purpose for pupils who feel they are mere obstacles to their freedom to seek jobs and earn a living.[5]

While Dr Finlay is referring to school pupils of low academic performance, his comments about the personal qualities of the museum educator are applicable to all classes. Appointing teachers of professional seniority to the museum service does not always meet these criteria. They have to initiate new learning experiences in an environment divorced from the classroom which are of a memorable quality, with children they do not know, and in a limited period of time. This calls for special qualities, as well as the stimulus which comes from mutual exchanges both at home and abroad.

Professional Training

Should education officers whose positions may be of limited tenure be given special training? Is such training provided in other countries, and, if so, at what level?

In Australia and New Zealand all education officers are trained teachers, and some are also university graduates. As Alison Heath[6] has pointed out, in England, America, Australia and New Zealand it appears to be generally accepted that the best preparation for a museum education officer is a degree in a relevant discipline, a teacher training certificate and considerable teaching experience, but that this form of qualification is not required internationally. Indeed, she states that in many countries a degree in art history appears to be the only requirement, although employment of people so qualified is often detrimental to their subsequent careers as teachers, both financially and professionally.

In Britain, according to Mrs Heath, both formal and informal training is also provided. Formal qualification is available through the Museums Association which has developed an in-service training scheme for museum officers of all

5. Ian Findlay, *Priceless Heritage: the Future of Museums, op.cit.*, p.98.
6. Alison M. Heath, 'The Training of Education Officers', in *Museum Education Training*: MEAA Conference, Sydney (April 1977), pp. 10–15.

disciplines, including education, who have completed a minimum of two years in full-time employment. This is a post-graduate qualification which has been obtained by some New Zealanders principally in the field of administration, but recent residential requirements in Britain now virtually place this out of reach.

Courses on museology in general are becoming more freely available but, generally speaking, education does not figure largely in the year's programme. Prescriptions for these courses resemble in general the ICOM Basic Syllabus for Museum Training, reprinted by Hudson[7] together with a list of places where such training courses are offered.[8] Hudson's list does not include Australia where several courses of this kind are available, the nearest being at the University of Sydney, and at Prahran College of Advanced Education, Melbourne. Because of the limited emphasis on education in such courses, a working party on training, set up by the International Council of Museums (ICOM) in 1969, has recently made recommendations on the qualifications, training facilities and status of museum education officers, and its report, taken from the Schools Council publication on museum education[9] appears in full in Appendix A. Clearly, these formal qualifications would be difficult to obtain from New Zealand and would not even be sought unless tenure was permanent, or career opportunities were attractive, although qualifications in this field are likely to be very valuable elsewhere.

Most countries rely on informal training through such activities as the conferences, seminars, and group training facilities run by the Group for Educational Services in Museums (GESM) in Britain;[10] or newsletters, surveys, and so on; or such activities as those of the Standing Professional Committee on Museum Education founded in 1973 under the auspices of the American Association of Museums;[11] or workshops and training sessions offered by the Canadian Museums Association and by provincial museum associations in Canada.[12]

In New Zealand some informal training is available. Newly appointed education officers who have no previous museum experience may, at the discretion of the district senior inspector, if they are to work in museums where they are the only teachers, be sent for orientation to another centre for periods ranging from a day to a week. Most have not found this adequate, as the work in another centre is often largely inappropriate to their own. The best way

7. Kenneth Hudson, *Museums for the 1980s: A Survey of World Trends* (Paris: Unesco, 1977), Appendix 5, pp.162-3.
8. *Ibid.*, pp.164-6.
9. *Pterodactyls and Old Lace, op.cit.*, pp.69-70.
10. *Museums and Children:* Monographs on Education, *op.cit.*, p.159.
11. *Ibid.*, Bonnie Pitman-Gelles, p.178, 9.
12. *Ibid.*, Maureen Gee, p.72.

many ideas can be transmitted is by group discussion, but at present education officers work in isolation from each other and most have never met. Conferences held biennially up to 1963, in conjunction with AGMANZ, were discontinued and, in consequence, museums as a whole have lost contact with the educational programmes operating throughout the country. An alternative would be a week of residential training at Lopdell House where such a course was held in 1972. Such courses are urgently needed and so is participation in AGMANZ Conferences, which provide a forum for discussing problems common to them all. Meanwhile, even an exchange of newletters would establish contact between centres, providing a platform from which appropriate measures could be taken to form their own professional association.

In Australia, biennial seminars in museum education have been held nationally since 1953, sponsored mainly by Unesco. A Museums Education Association of Australia (MEAA) was formed in 1975. Their conferences, to which key speakers are brought from overseas, enable them to meet and participate in professional discussions of a stimulating nature. Their published seminar reports are a valuable resource on museum education, showing not only the rapid proliferation of museum services throughout Australia but also progressive emphasis on training, research and publication. We would have much to gain, nationally, by forming a similar group within New Zealand and by association with this Australian group.

Relationship of Education Officers to Teachers Colleges

From 1941-65 education officers were administratively attached to the staffs of local teachers colleges, facilitating organization for student training as well as services in the form of museum clubs, facilities for academic courses, and exercises by professional studies staffs working with students' and children's groups.

Some education officers and museum staff members accompanied student parties in activity weeks. In Otago the education officer, Les Lockerbie who was also an anthropologist, took students to work on early Maori field sites, and in Wellington the museum entomologist, Ron Ordish, accompanied student parties to Great Barrier Island for several successive years.

Severance of Education Officers from Teachers Colleges

At an AGMANZ Conference in 1961 the education officers made appeals to the Department of Education representative, Walter B. Harris, for salary equ-

A museum of technology comes to life. Education officer, student teachers and children watching an old hay baler in operation (Photo: MOTAT).

ation with teachers college lecturers on the grounds of their heavy involvement with student teacher training. They claimed to be working with approximately 20 students at a time, a number far in excess of those allocated to each normal school teacher. The time spent in this discussion was considered excessive by the Department of Education and they were no longer given leave to attend biennial conferences of AGMANZ from 1963. They were transferred administratively to the staffs of local normal schools in 1965 and given an extra allowance for training student teachers.

The present attachment to normal schools is far less satisfactory because of the loss of professional initiatives engendered between the colleges and the museums. As George Guy, the first education officer at Canterbury Museum and later Principal of Christchurch Teachers College, pointed out, earlier education officers furnished monthly reports to their principals and participated in staff meetings, providing better communication and knowledge about museum resources for the colleges. The practice of furnishing these reports gradually lapsed and much of the present isolation of the education officers is due to lack of regular communication between them and other educational bodies. Most of the people interviewed in this survey regarded the close relationship between both institutions as a strength with lasting benefits to the students.

The move has also had other profound and unexpected effects, which will be described later in the section on teachers colleges.

Relationship of Education Officers to Museum Staffs

Museum education officers are not members of the museum staffs and this is professionally isolating. There is also friction about salary, conditions of work and holidays. Their working hours isolate them from the social moments the staff shares, because they have to be available by telephone before and after school and during the lunch hour, and because teaching in the galleries often coincides with the morning tea break.

Education officers are dependent on the good will of the museum staffs to be able to work effectively. On appointment they face the need to become familiar with the history and significance of the museum collections, and much of this they get personally from the museum staff. The degree to which they are included in meetings on policy and display varies between institutions and is a question of courtesy and not of right. Smaller staffs find it easier to meet and work together. In larger institutions the separation is more apparent and they are not always included in policy discussions and planning, which is regrettable as it is important that they should participate in the critically important planning for museum displays where they have a contribution to make. They use the displays more than do the professional staff, and they also see the reaction of the public to them.

It is the education officer who is likely to discover that children below a certain height cannot see some exhibits and has to hold the children up or provide platforms for them to see, or that the labels are confusing or too erudite and has to translate them. As the type of display which he would like to use may conflict with the opinion of the museum staff, the lack of opportunity to influence planning can be a real problem. At times displays may be removed without his knowledge and classes who have booked may arrive and find themselves confronted by bare or dismantled cases.

The separation also tends to divert the attention of the museum staff from educational activities, unless the director is pursuing a vigorous educational policy. There is a gap between school programmes and those for adults which are principally meetings of scientific societies traditionally associated with museums. Effective programmes for children and adults should be on-going and planned in consultation. The separation is widened by the disappointing attitude of education officers who limit their hours of work to those of the schools and who remain apart from general museum activities.

Education officers in Australia describe similar difficulties. Some feel their work with children is largely a palliative exercise to take the pressure of their demands from the museum staffs: 'We are just here to get them off their backs.' Many feel that working with children is regarded as of less significance than research programmes. Grafting a service for children run by the education authorities on to the traditional structure of a museum is not entirely satisfactory. But it is less of a problem where the majority of education staff are appointed directly to the staff of the museum, have a voice in determining policy, and are familiar with the range of objectives of other professional staff.

A different attitude is reported by Victoria Airey in her summary of 84 museum education services in Great Britain and Northern Ireland. She states:

> Curatorial attitudes some years ago of suspicion towards museum education services have now generally been replaced by positive cooperation and the common viewpoint of the museum as a provider of a public service. Most authorities see an education service both as a necessary and a prestige service.[13]

This appears to be the outcome of a sustained analysis of museum education services by a series of reports from 1963 onwards which Airey describes[14] and which have led to the establishment of new services with wider responsibility and potential, vigorously facilitating cross-currents of ideas and information. She further points out that this change in attitude has led to much greater awareness of the educational potential of museums and that, in recent years, some museum education officers have become directors of museums.

Opportunities for Professional Exchange

It would help to break down the present very damaging sense of isolation, which many education officers seem to feel, if they could meet more fre-

13. *Museums and Children:* Monographs on Education, *op.cit.*, p.162.
14. *Ibid.*, p.157.

quently, have access to more literature about their work, and have the stimulus of overseas experience. Proposals to exchange museum teachers with overseas counterparts have been approved when these have been negotiated privately beforehand. In 1949 there was an exchange between Otago Museum and the American Museum of Natural History (AMNH), and, although the American teacher failed to arrive because of other teaching commitments, the Otago staff member worked for over a year in AMNH, helped in travel costs by the Fulbright Exchange Scheme. In 1956 a similar exchange took place between the National Museum and the Geoffrye Museum, London. While each was responsible for her own fare, the London teacher was helped by the British Museums Association. Positions and salaries were interchanged.

A report from the English teacher, Olive Royston, was published in the *Museums Journal* in 1958.[15] Exchange teachers can make a special contribution to each museum and provide a better degree of understanding than short visits. Workable arrangements are more likely to be found in museums of the same size.

While exchanges have traditionally been directed towards North American and European museums, consideration should now be given to other areas. A report by Dr R.K. Dell on his participation in the Unesco Regional Seminar, Tokyo and Kyoto, March 1976, emphasizes the high professional standards of Asian museums which, he says, in many areas are ahead of those in New Zealand. Under General Remarks, he lists some main fields in which he thinks New Zealand would best contribute, and of these one is our museum education system, especially at the primary school level. He recommends that 'endeavours should be made to initiate exchange between senior staff members of New Zealand and Asian Museums, especially in the fields of museum education and scientific research and that exchanges with Japan would possibly be the easiest to establish'.[16]

Professional Support

Each district senior inspector or his representative in the inspectorate has responsibility for local support, and the help these busy men give to these services is highly commendable. The establishment of advisory committees which inform and coordinate locally, as well as some procedures for extended visits, have been initiatives from such men.

15. Olive Royston, 'A Visit to New Zealand', in *Museums Journal*, London, Vol. 57, No. 10 (January 1958), pp. 231-3.
16. Report on Unesco Regional Seminar, Tokyo and Kyoto, 22-27 March 1976. Summarized in *AGMANZ NEWS*, Auckland, Vol. 7, No. 3 (August 1976), pp. 45-7.

Despite good local support, lack of coordination between education board districts is the cause of failure to gain consensus on policy on a national basis. While in theory museum educational services are discussed at conferences of the district senior inspectors, in practice their first attention must be given to the needs of the schools, and museum issues may not be given adequate discussion because of lack of time. The failure to define policy or to pursue initiatives from the district to national levels is an important influence adversely affecting the day-to-day functioning of museum education services.

Morale is low among serving education officers whose position is an unenviable one. The factors adversely affecting them are:

(1) Isolation both from museums and schools.

(2) Lack of professional support and recognition.

(3) Decline in salary and status levels in the school system.

(4) Lack of policy guidelines.

(5) Failure to enlist support from existing educational organizations.

(6) Lack of leadership and opportunity to form their own articulate group.

(7) Lack of opportunity for professional exchange.

While the Department of Education has yielded to strong local pressures since 1965 to staff 9 additional provincial institutions, it has failed at the same time to provide an implemented policy on educational goals, financial support, professional encounters or special training. Lack of contact has so limited exchanges about teaching programmes that brilliant work being done in several museums is largely unknown elsewhere, although greater contact would be the most effective way of improving the quality of their work. Encouragement is needed for those whose hard work, and well-planned and innovative efforts have not received recognition.

To whom can they look for support? They are no longer part of the teachers colleges, nor are all attached to the same type of school; in fact, the part-time education officers at Invercargill and Napier are not attached directly to a local school. On a local basis they can approach the DSIs, but when they have attempted to move through them from local to national level, to apply for example, for Lopdell House training, or a rationale for funding operating expenses, they have been unable to get a reply. They have been mentioned only once in 40 years in the E-1 Report of the Department of Education. Hopes have been raised by the surveys carried out in 1969 and 1975 by the Department of Education but these have not been made public, nor have the recommendations they contain been actioned. As education officers do not meet, they have so far not attempted to form their own association.

In its survey of museum education services in 1975, the Department of

Education noted that lecture-type lessons were becoming increasingly common. It stated that many of the museum programmes appeared to place the children in a situation where they were talked at and directed to static displays, and that most education officers seemed to see the museum service as a means of disseminating information. It recommended that the education officers be given training to improve the quality of the museum experiences, to emphasize the importance of allowing children to handle materials, and to develop their skills in involving children in the enquiry approach.

It was thought that much of the pre-visit preparation and follow-up work was left to chance. More staffing to provide more systematic previsit teaching and follow up activities was suggested. Other recommendations included:

(1) An investigation of staggered leave time to allow staffing of museums in school holidays.

(2) Initiatives to meet the needs of special groups.

(3) Visits to schools by the education officers to take lessons, participate in staff meetings, and to share planning.

(4) A Lopdell House or residential course in the near future.

(5) A change in the school loan system to kits of slides, tape cassettes, overhead transparencies, artefacts or replicas.

Innovations and changes noted were:

(1) More teachers beginning to use museums themselves.

(2) Work with gifted children briefed on material for selected topics at Canterbury Museum.

(3) Visits of Canterbury Museum education officers to schools for half-days in 1974.

(4) Residential 2-3 day classes on selected Maori topics at Gisborne.

(5) Extended visits of up to a week including painting and drama at Otago Museum.

The contents of this report and its recommendations delineate the innovative aspects of current services as well as current weaknesses. If adopted, the measures it suggests would provide much needed professional support and guidance.

Since the early 1950s education officers have appealed to NZEI to investigate and support their claims of loss of salary and status relativities. On our enquiring about the most recent claim, we discovered only that in 1971 and 1979 sub-committees compared the relativities of museum officers with other unspecified special services. Documents detailing these were not available, and recommendations made to the NZEI Executive Council were said to be recorded in confidential minutes. No action was ever taken.

The most consistent support for education officers has come from AGMANZ, which in January 1969 appealed to the Director-General of Education for discussion of the effect on museum services of the withdrawal of student teachers from teaching in the galleries, under Three Year Training. J.M. Wisely, DSI, Wanganui Education Board, duly attended the AGMANZ Conference of April 1969 to discuss this matter with the council.[17]

Then, following further representations, approval and assistance were given to nine North Island education officers and five school inspectors to attend the New Plymouth AGMANZ Conference in 1975, which had a workshop theme, 'Museum Education: A Specialized Field'. Unfortunately, no report was tabled, nor were policy guidelines forwarded to AGMANZ Council from this meeting. South Island education officers attended the following conference in Dunedin, in 1977, when S. Waterman, education officer at MOTAT, presented a paper.[18] But no other initiatives were recorded.

It has remained for an independent research organization, NZCER, to undertake this survey partly funded by the McKenzie Education Foundation, and using the services of a retired teacher.

Our conclusions are that the earlier experimental services funded by Carnegie Corporation and administered by NZCER set world standards for that time in recommending:

(1) That public galleries be used to teach children how to use museums. Where these were unsuitably arranged, the museums proceeded to upgrade them.

(2) That provisions be made to extend these experiences into leisure-time activities.

(3) That handling materials be provided for children to examine.

(4) That instruction be given in small groups to facilitate discussion and examination of artefacts.

(5) That student teachers be trained in the use of museum resources.

Teaching in the galleries, provision of handling materials and opportunities for leisure activities are now standard practice in most other countries. While instruction in small groups is generally regarded as the ideal, most classes elsewhere appear to be taught as a whole. Individual museums and colleges of education now run training courses in the use of museum resources, but the

17. See Appendix B for an account of this conference.
18. Stafford M. Waterman, 'Museums as Educational Partners', in *AGMANZ News,* Auckland, Vol. 8, No. 2 (May 1977), pp. 21-4.

New Zealand system continues to be the only nationally based system of this kind in the world.

To regain levels comparable with those of other developed countries a reorganization of existing services is urgently needed.

Children in the care of a student teacher during a lesson on pioneer buildings (Photo: MOTAT).

6   Teachers Colleges and Museums

> Your museum liaison system is in fact something we have been regarding as the desirable ideal for years. Your young teachers go into the museums for a period, help the museum staff, become familiar with what is there and then take the children round *in small groups* . . . which is what the expert museum staff can never spare time to do. Then they go out and spread their knowledge further. In other countries this is being urged as a fundamental step. But here you have had it going for eight years and it's a fine example. I think perhaps people don't appreciate what a fine thing you have here.

This extract is taken from a reported interview with Dr Grace McCann Morley, President of the American Association of Art Museum Directors, Director of the San Francisco Museum of Art, by Anthony Alpers in 1956.[1] When viewed over 20 years later, the last words have a prophetic ring.

The close association between teachers colleges and museum education services established in 1938 has already been described in Chapter 2. The dimensions of this plan, devised by Dr Gilbert Archey in the Auckland War Memorial Museum, have become increasingly evident during this survey as problems relating to museum activities with children and comparable systems in other countries have been examined. Built into it was a combination of the use of museum resources, the needs of the schools, the training of young teachers and provision for a means of reducing the adult-child ratio in the museum galleries. It was aimed at both the immediate needs of children and also at provision for the education of a new body of teachers familiar with the aims and workings of a museum. In 1956, the same year as Dr Morley visited New Zealand, the ICOM Committee for Education published, with the assistance of Unesco, a handbook, *Museums and Teachers* , describing the various training schemes for teachers in the use of museum resources, which were operating in the Western World. It was not intended to be a definitive analysis of all methods, but in the Introduction, Hannah T. Rose, Chairman, Education Committee of ICOM, states:

1. Anthony Alpers, 'High Praise for Our Museums', in *Home and Building* (New Zealand) 1 April 1956.

The feeling of the majority of museum education staffs and of educational authorities is that in order to be most effective such training must be incorporated in the regular curriculum of training colleges and schools of education in order to reach potential teachers at the young, formative stage.[2]

The section, 'Teachers in Training', is divided into 'Courses on a National Basis' and 'Courses on a Local Basis', and from this we see that New Zealand alone provided on a national basis for this type of training. The detailed description of the scheme which had been supplied by the New Zealand Department of Education has been widely quoted and applauded as an ideal. It has been interesting to see how often one part in particular has been quoted,[3] references to it appearing in writings up to 1978.

> Students are told, 'You are not here to teach a lesson, nor to tell all you know, nor to give all the answers. Your duty is not so much to tell as to ask; not so much to fix facts as to invite hypothesis. Your task is to help the children appreciate, at their own level, the significance of the exhibits, to arouse wonder and curiosity, to ask questions, to propound problems and to challenge their powers of reasoning. You are not required to fill the child's ears with words but to open his mind to new experiences.

Following the publication of this booklet, a steady stream of experts from overseas, interested in examining this scheme, was recorded in the annual reports of the museums concerned.

At present, this training is reduced, a drying-up process which began some 10 years ago with the introduction of Three Year Training.

The changes which affected museums were:

(1) The reduction in the total number of weeks in which students were sent out to schools for teaching practice.

(2) The structuring of those postings to the study of specific teaching classroom skills and aspects of children's development.

The most puzzling part of this survey has been the search for the administrative or professional decisions related to museum education services when the colleges moved into Three Year Training. As Rhys Griffiths, Education Officer at Canterbury Museum, 1958-60, said nostalgically of this period: 'Those were the golden years. The schools loved you, the colleges loved you, everyone loved you. You couldn't put a foot wrong. I wonder what went wrong?' As he indicated, in the early 1960s, museum services appeared to have reached a highly successful peak (Tables A1, A7). Attendance figures were continuing to rise; the colleges were entrusting more and more students to them for training, and the interest shown in their work, and the visits from overseas

---

2. *Museums and Teachers*, ICOM Committee for Education (Paris: ICOM, 1956), p.12.
3. *Ibid.*, p.16.

museum educators, were both gratifying and intoxicating. Yet as each college in turn moved into the new pattern of training, the use of museums was virtually dropped, an unexpected and baffling phenomenon which has never been explained. Because of this, some detail is appropriate and can be found in Appendix B.

Even after Three Year Training, we still find that other countries were still urging this museum service as a desirable aim, which had not developed beyond schemes offered by individual institutions, such as the Victoria and Albert scheme described by Renée Marcousé in *Animation and Information* in 1969. From Britain in *Museums in Education*, we read:

> The most effective long-term method of interesting people in museums and in using their contents is through the schools. Yet it is possible to go through school, college and university and never visit a museum nor be encouraged to use one. This generalized statement applies almost equally to those who are in training as teachers. In all colleges of education and university departments of education, some teaching about the resources and use of museums should be given.
>
> To enable some serving teachers to gain an understanding of how to use museums, they ought to be seconded to museums for periods ranging from a few weeks to the semi-permanent arrangements of the ILEA, Liverpool and other authorities.[4]

Papers from a conference on museum education in the USA, *Museums and Education*, edited by Eric Larrabee, 1968, list recommendations for all student teachers to spend some time during training in studying and working in museums as well as in-service courses, with credit, for practising teachers.

Effect on Museum Teaching Programmes of the Reduction in Student Postings

When Three Year Training was introduced, school services were still confined to the four main museums, and from Table A7 it is interesting to see that, rather than the expected drop, the usual annual increase in attendances continued after 1967. As the changeover to this type of training was staggered through the country, immediate effects on all four museums would not be expected. In a number of museums the increased attendance was catered for by handing over more responsibility to the class teachers, many of whom, particularly in Otago, conduct their own classes after advice from the museum education staff. Credit must also be given to the education officers, some of whom met the situation by training groups of volunteers to help regularly. Some use parents, as already mentioned. In Christchurch, an additional assistant was seconded to the staff. At present, large classes are slotted into the weeks when students will be

4. *Museums in Education:* Education Survey, No. 12, *op.cit.*, p.44.

available, and smaller classes are taken with the help of the class teachers and any students who happen to accompany the visiting class. The class teacher, as the education officers decided at their Lopdell House course in 1972, has been brought in more. Despite this, the number of children in each group being taken round museum galleries has reached excessively high numbers and much of the teaching pattern has reverted to the lecture and instructional type of lesson rather than the discovery situation.

An important advance has been the involvement of the class teacher, which solved a weakness in the former system. What used to be known unofficially as the 'package deal' was a system in which museums sent out a list of possible lessons, one or two of which were selected by a class. The whole visit was in the hands of the museum staff and students, from the introduction to the final film session. Teachers remained apart from the activities, some even taking advantage of this to slip away on private affairs, a situation known in many countries. The present arrangement, where the class teacher and museum officers discuss and plan the coming lessons together, is greatly superior.

Selection and Training of Students

Organization was fairly simple. Education officers were attached to the staffs of the local teachers college where the museum was listed as a practice school. As a special posting, it was given only on request, but the list of students applying for this was usually lengthy. Generally, only students who were expected to perform well (as all their teaching was done in public galleries) were allocated, but in later years it was occasionally used unobtrusively for some insecure students, particularly those who had encountered difficulties in control. This aspect was not generally known, partly to protect the students, and also to prevent an image forming that the museum section was being used for 'ambulance cases'. That this could occur showed the confidence of the staff of the teachers colleges in the quality of training being given to their students, and affirms that the training and help given was of a quality which enabled them to reach good levels of performance. Museums have a responsibility to visiting classes which have expended time and money preparing for the visit, and poor teaching in these circumstances is unacceptable. But the small, intimate group of 6-8 children, working with a student teacher in the galleries, examining displays, handling and exploring materials, asking endless questions, discussing and arguing is ideal for the young teacher who wishes to relate to children, gain confidence, and develop teaching skills. The group size of 6-8 children is considered to be optimum.

Training still conforms to a common pattern. The first week of the posting is

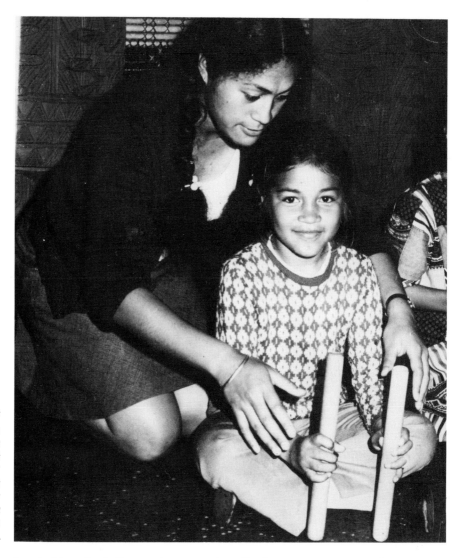

devoted to orientation and preparation. Students visit museum departments not normally open to the public, receive information about the selected collections they are to use, and are introduced to the aims of museum teaching. The significance and power of using a direct source of discovery open to children of all ages, and without the use of written language, underlies all their training.

A strength is the evaluation which occurs among the students when a class leaves, because all have shared a common experience. In the school situation, most students are on their own and evaluation is between student and associate teacher. In the museum, once a class has left and the gallery tidied, students rush to their room, brew up their coffee and exchange lively accounts about the children they have just taught. Unusual reactions, awkward questions, are shared spontaneously. The education officer is buttonholed for more information, perhaps for advice, perhaps for sympathy. At this point they may be told that the departing class was classified as of low academic performance, and this always evokes much astonishment and discussion. Such children are often so responsive and discuss the exciting objects about them so perceptively that it is difficult to believe that they come from low stream classes. Young teachers are thus shown a new way of interesting and stimulating children whose handicap may be that of difficulty with written language. Unlike the classroom practice, in the museum the lesson will be repeated many times. Students become confident with the materials and are able to concentrate more on their techniques of teaching. Children are the variable and students suddenly understand something of individual differences — how widely they differ and how unpredictable their responses may be. Tape recorders and videotape may be used to help them evaluate their own performance.

It is customary for the education officer to take the whole class in an introductory session and later to summarize and discuss what has been seen. After the introduction, the students each with 6-8 children, conduct their groups through the galleries, examining a sequence of displays and using handling material related to the topic. Staff from the teachers college visit the museum to observe and evaluate each student's performance. The number of their visits at each posting depends on how many students are present, and the degree of help needed. Evaluations by the education officer are also sent to the college, and the students take away with them a section book recording the work of the three- or four-week period.

Value of Museum Sections

Opinions about the value of these have been sought from museum directors, teachers college staffs, district senior inspectors, museum education officers, past students and students on section in Auckland in November 1978. The tracing of all 9,000 past students was too complicated a task, but over 200 were encountered during the course of the study in many situations, from a recently retired teacher, who was in the first experimental batch at the National Museum in 1938, onwards.

The enthusiasm of most students for this experience has constantly been noted, but evidence of the long-term effects was also sought. Former students, now widely scattered through various education services, include a number of

museum directors and professional staff who earlier trained as teachers and who had these museum sections. Many former students are now serving on museum advisory committees, some are liaison officers between museums and teachers colleges, primary or secondary schools, and serve on museum management committees, showing, by their efforts to promote educational activity in the museum, a continued interest which they felt had originated in their museum sections. Those who happen to be in the school inspectorate bring more support and a greater degree of understanding to this work which is directly under their supervision. Many who are teaching bring in their classes independently; indeed, some students in subsequent sections also bring in classes, and by conducting them themselves in this by now familiar environment, can choose a suitable time for the visit without waiting for an appointment.

Of those interviewed, 3 percent expressed dissatisfaction with the whole concept of museum service, the reasons which they gave being lack of involvement and insufficient work to do on section. As opinions from past students at the same institutions, but under other education officers, were favourable, it would seem that such dissatisfaction was a personal rather than an organizational matter. Although the percentage of critics was low, their comments should be examined carefully, as it includes a museum director, an assistant director, a DSI, senior teachers college staff members and executive members of NZEI. While successful museum sections appear to engender continued support and interest, the consequences of unsatisfactory museum sections may be equally far-reaching.

The second criticism, offered frequently, was the lack of continued contact with children, so that a closer relationship was not possible, although it was not considered sufficient grounds for discontinuing museum postings. Most past students say the same thing, 'It was the best section I ever had'. A number still had their section books, and expressed continued interest in subjects they had first studied in the museum. Some who were still class teachers either took their own classes to the museum, or in less direct ways indicated their interest. Some analytical interviews were obtained as well.

The advantages they listed were:

(1) Access to such a wide range of children, who came from all city as well as country areas. 'Where else would you get the chance to meet so many different kinds of children? I think only an inspector at the end of his career could claim to have had an equal opportunity. They came from all over the place and you really knew what "they" meant when "they" talked about individual differences. It was something I never forgot.'

(2) The micro-teaching situation where the number of variables present in a classroom situation is reduced. There are few discipline problems; the group with the student is always small; interest level is high; repetition enables the student to become familiar with the lesson content, freeing him to concentrate on teaching techniques; repetition with another group enables students to overcome poor strategies without the embarrassment of facing the same children again; it is particularly helpful to students with a low level of confidence; questioning techniques and discovery methods are given intensive attention.

(3) The opportunity to use a resource outside the education system.

(4) The need continually to upgrade one's knowledge. Whatever scepticism students may express on this point, it remains true that over the 40 years of the scheme's existence students have enjoyed the challenge demanded of them. Children's questions continually show up gaps in their knowledge, which a single lesson may not do in the classroom. Moreover, as their knowledge grows, so do their pride and interest in it.

(5) The team-teaching situation, where students have more say in structuring the lessons. They find this satisfying, as they do the spontaneous, informal evaluation that follows, because it is a group effort.

(6) Opportunity to handle some museum specimens, to get to know

museum staff, and to explore the workrooms of the museums. Many students experience a sense of satisfaction in their temporary involvement with museum staff, an association which fails to develop in the same way in a lecture-type situation.

(7) Involvement with a primary source of knowledge. As this comes only when the allocated time is blocked to 3 or 4 weeks, the short visit of student groups to learn about museum services fails entirely to establish it. Such an involvement imparts to many young students the sense of wonder and the excitement of discovery which is the ultimate aim of all museums.

(8) Opportunity to use teaching aids of dramatic quality. 'The things were so exciting in themselves, I learnt to get out of the way and let them and the children get together. There was no need of the strong-eye stuff in front of the group to keep them in order. I learnt the value of the low-key approach from behind the group, just to help them see the most important things. I almost always work from behind my classes even now, and have often wondered how long it would have taken me to get this if I had not had a museum section. Certainly I would have done so, but I think I came to it several years earlier because of this experience.'

(9) Opportunity to see children of low academic performance in a new setting. Children from low-stream classes in a museum situation frequently cannot be distinguished from children of a high performance level. Many education officers do not speak about this to the students before such visits, but wait to reveal it in the general discussion afterwards.

(10) Gain in confidence expressed by many students. The important factor in the success of the scheme has been *the period of time spent at the museum*, which must be long enough for students to begin to identify with the institution. This appears to be four weeks. The same feelings are not engendered by visits of short duration, even if these are frequent or if they total equivalent hours. Perhaps to experience this it is necessary to pass through the door labelled 'Staff only' for a while in one's own right to have this feeling of belonging.

Criticisms expressed:

(1) Lack of opportunity to get to know children individually.

(2) Lack of time to form satisfactory relationships with children.

(3) Boredom with repetition of lessons.

(4) Lack of opportunity to accompany classes back to schools.

Use of Museums by Teachers College Staffs

Of recent years more experimental use has been made of museums in Auckland and Wellington for activities with students and school classes by teachers college staffs. Professional studies staffs have mounted exercises where students plan and accompany classes on excursions to the museum. Beginning with preparation in classrooms, these require a visit to the museum before the one made with the children, participation with follow-up work in schools, and later evaluation at the college. Social studies staffs have applied new methods in practical teaching to their area of the school curriculum, mainly for second-year students. Of these, the most sustained came from the Social Studies Department of North Shore Teachers College under the guidance of its principal lecturer, John Buckland, who used the museum for three-week postings for second-year students. Several important features of his programme are noted:

(1) Bookings of classes are made by the college from schools in its study area, in consultation with the museum staff's timetable of gallery usage.

(2) One or two students from the group visit the school, meet the children and find out the stage to which the classroom study has progressed.

(3) All students then combine to plan the lesson to suit the school's needs. The basis for planning is a team-teaching effort.

(4) Teaching strategy is based on a multi-sensory approach, including role-playing, music, dancing, manipulation, food sampling, dressing up, study of social customs, and examination of social patterns of various ethnic and early cultures. Extensive use is made of the museum classroom to prepare dramatic settings.

(5) Students remain with a small group, move from one activity to another in the museum classroom, accompanied by a student partner, and conclude by examining appropriate gallery exhibits.

(6) Two students accompany the class back to school to participate in the follow-up work.

(7) Throughout, the students are in the care of a lecturer from the college who works full-time in the museum for the weeks this needs. This programme, which has been operating successfully for five years, requires good personal relationships between college, museum and museum education staff. The same system operates in MOTAT under another lecturer.[5] Before the end of the section, museum education staff

5. Stafford M. Waterman, 'International Year of the Child: North Shore Teachers College Students on Teaching Section at the Museum of Transport and Technology', in *AGMANZ News*, Auckland, Vol. 10, No. 2 (May 1979), pp.7-8.

provide an independent evaluation of the quality of teaching of each student.

A number of suggestions, principally related to variations in academic studies or teaching practice, has been made for fuller use of museums by the teachers colleges. The most innovative is a suggestion to include museum studies as a subject in its own right in the college curriculum from which students select their academic studies. This would necessitate the appointment of a lecturer in museum studies to the college staff to teach courses which would operate at first-, second-, and third-year levels. This idea has also been aired in Great Britain.

> We can train teachers for museum work if we want to do it. We can put on courses for backward readers, for environmental studies, for practical mathematics. It is a matter of priorities. It may be that a museum course should be one of a wide range of options put on by colleges of education so that students with natural interests and enthusiasm for the work would be able to choose this opportunity to learn to use the museum well.[6]

6. *Pterodactyls and Old Lace:* Museums in Education, *op.cit.,* pp.68, 69.

The small, intimate group is ideal for the young teacher to learn to relate to children (Photo: National Museum).

Teaching strategy based on a multi-sensory approach. Re-enactment of a kava ceremony (Photo: John Buckland).

With autonomy, each college is free to adapt its programmes towards a fuller use of museum resources. Possible developments which have been discussed with Wellington Teachers College include:

(1) Transfer of the museum education officer to the staff of the college.

(2) Appointment of a lecturer in museum studies to the staff of the college.

(3) Establishment of full-time training courses at certificate level for museum education officers.

(4) Courses for student teachers in the use of museum resources, similar to those for selected studies at first-, second-, and third-year levels for the Diploma in Teaching.

(5) Short, practical courses in museum teaching within the professional studies curriculum.

(6) Courses for trained teachers at Stages I and II for the Advanced Diploma in Teaching in the use of museum resources.

7   What Is Being Left Out

The scope of this survey has been restricted to a limited section of museum educational activity, that is, to those services which are staffed by trained teachers appointed to specified museums by the Department of Education. One would therefore expect that their attention would be directed mainly to the services which relate closely to school practice.

In suggesting areas of activity which are being overlooked, we are not attempting to define the total educational potential of these museums but rather to indicate either where alternative activities have lapsed or have been developed in other countries, principally in Australia, by education staff similarly deployed from the Department of Education.

Alternative and expanded services may readily be suggested. The problem is always to decide on the emphasis which each service should be given, because feasible and appropriate developments may yet put undue demands on existing museum resources. The proliferation of education services in a museum usually requires comparable development in other areas, for example, more staff, rooms, handling materials, reference materials, displays, public facilities and finance. New Zealand museums are not well-endowed financially, and have to balance their resources between the needs of their functions of collection, conservation and research as well as education. The most important omission in the past has been provision for regular informal discussion between museum directors and education authorities.

The last time these two groups met to discuss their mutual roles and assess their expanding services was in May 1941 when the Department of Education took over responsibility for staffing this work. The minutes from this meeting, summarized on pp. 18, 19, could well be used to open the next, as they indicate that a broader use of museum resources was then initially intended. Such expectations were based on the early experimental work during 1938-40, which deliberately ranged widely in order to evaluate the effectiveness of different methods of approach, and was the subject of comment in the 1939 NZCER report to the Carnegie Corporation, where the difficulties in balancing the disposal of time between activities were pointed out.

If services are to be diversified, this may have to be done at the expense of some of those currently emphasized, and decisions related to diversification should be made by consultation between both parties. A comment in papers from a conference on museum education in the United States[1] is pertinent to this issue. It states:

> The group also saw a danger strictly as a dog on a leash, in the expanding of present new developments in the school curriculum. We felt that the museums should expand by their own standards rather than by those set by any other institution, although of course in full harmony and cooperation with other institutions (this is the same matter as defending the museum's independence as an educational institution in its own right).

It should be recognized that both museums and the Department of Education have separate educational functions which may fruitfully overlap. Friction both here and in other countries appears to be caused by a lack of knowledge of each other's objectives because of the absence of dialogue between them. In this country, the aims of both parties appear to have diverged. Those of the officers of the Department of Education appear to be directed exclusively at the enrichment of school studies by visits to the museum or by use of its loan resources. Although no restriction is placed on the age levels catered for, services operate most intensively with children of primary school age, gradually diminishing at intermediate and secondary school levels. Initiatives with teacher training, and so on, are directed towards similar ends.

The aims expressed by museum directors, as discussed elsewhere, are directed at assisting children to use these institutions for their own personal enrichment to help establish patterns which will remain in adult life. Museum writings emphasize the analogy between teaching children to use and enjoy museums and teaching them to use and enjoy libraries. Directors generally expressed satisfaction with the work for schools and dissatisfaction with the fact that most education officers do not regard the 'recreational' or voluntary activities as their responsiblity. Such activities are believed to have more lasting effects and to 'stir the sense of the marvellous' in the child to a greater degree.

Evaluation and Research

Some of the most striking developments in imaginative and constructive use of museums described in Unesco's *Museums and Children*[2] are taking place in

1. Eric Larrabee, ed., *Museums and Education*. Papers from conference held at University of Vermont, August 21-6, 1966 (Washington DC.: Smithsonian Institution Press, 1968), p.232.
2. 'Museums and Children', in *Museum*, Vol. XXXI, No. 3, 1979.

countries faced with widespread problems of illiteracy and general education, and it is thought-provoking to see how carefully evaluated and assessed their programmes are when compared with the easy-going ways in which our museum resources are used. Little effort has been made here to appraise and evaluate existing programmes, although this is now an accepted part of the procedure followed when new initiatives are tried out in many other countries.

The amount of published material in New Zealand in the past 40 years is pitifully small. Apart from the already mentioned *Educating in Five Dimensions*[3] by H.W. Beaumont, who was education officer at Canterbury Museum, 1945-58, there is little to show. Five undergraduate or graduate theses and one research paper have been written, four of which evaluated some activity and two were purely descriptive. School loan cases and problems of their distribution was the subject in 1954 of a thesis for the Diploma of the Museums Association, Great Britain, by J.C. Hall,[4] who in 1953-4 undertook an enquiry into the effectiveness of student training.[5] Evaluation of aspects of museum teaching techniques was carried out by G.G. Dearnley[6] at the Dominion (National) Museum, and A.W. Scott[7] at the Auckland War Memorial Museum as part requirements for university degrees in education. The two descriptive theses by V.F. Fisher[8] and T.T. Barrow[9] give useful accounts of services current in 1946 and 1954 respectively, that of Fisher giving an interesting insight into some of the early work in Auckland for handicapped people. None of these seems to have appeared in published form.

Evaluation can help to put educational work on a sounder basis, not only as a purely rational activity but also when determined by feelings and other reactions pertaining to the emotional sphere. As Ger van Wengen, President of the ICOM Committee for Education and Cultural Action (CECA), points out,[10] in recent years more specific expertise has been brought to bear on both planning and evaluation procedures, recognizing the need for scientific underpinning of

3. *op.cit.*
4. J.C. Hall, 'School Loan Cases and Problems of their Distribution in New Zealand with Special Reference to the Dominion Museum', thesis for the Diploma of the Museums Association, Great Britain, 1954.
5. J.C. Hall, 'Survey of Museum Services at the Dominion Museum with Enquiry into the Effectiveness of Student Teacher Training', unpublished, 1953-4 (mimeo).
6. G.G. Dearnley, 'An Evaluation of Some Aspects of the Educational Value of the Dominion Museums School Service in Wellington City Area', MA education thesis, 1947 (Victoria University of Wellington).
7. A.W. Scott, 'School Children and the Museum', MA education thesis, 1952 (Auckland University).
8. V.F. Fisher, 'An Analysis of the Educational Work in New Zealand Museums', MA, education thesis, 1946 (Auckland University).
9. T.T. Barrow, 'A Survey of the Organization and Administration of Education in the New Zealand Museums and Art Galleries', MA education thesis, 1954 (Victoria University of Wellington).
10. 'Introduction', in *Museum*, Vol. XXXI, No. 3 (1979), p.152.

museum educational programmes. In emphasizing that evaluation requires the aid of specially trained staff he states:

> Another important task that requires the aid of specially trained experts is evaluation of educational programmes. The better we are able to assess the results of our programmes, the better we shall know how and where such programmes possibly need to be supplemented or modified. Evaluation is no simple matter, particularly as far as the affective consequences of educational programmes are concerned.

Few of our services are staffed sufficiently to include specially trained personnel in these procedures, but recognition of this need, the keeping of data, records of opinions, and so on, would be a beginning. Pooling resources could provide a basis from which work could be undertaken. The present isolation and consequent fragility of museum education services could be countered, strengthened and supported by engaging the interest of research organizations whose advice would be helpful and whose documentation would provide useful publicity and recognition.

In Australia expert help for objective appraisal of existing services and experimental projects is being provided by the universities. For example, the University of New South Wales and the University of Sydney,[11] respectively, are evaluating two current programmes at the Australian Museum in Sydney, while the Victoria Science Museum and the University of Melbourne have jointly looked at the problem of the integration of the community's educational resources, and appropriate evaluation procedures.[12] Similar efforts in New Zealand to obtain expert assistance and enlist professional support from the universities or research organizations would be most desirable.

Leisure Activities

Preoccupation with school classes whose visits so satisfyingly clock up large attendance figures diverts attention from the relatively small numbers of children who come in of their own accord in leisure time. How are we to know what children derive from these visits or what the motives are which bring them into the building? Some reminiscent descriptions by adults of their early childhood visits to museums, collected by Kenneth Hudson,[13] reveal a romantic and imaginative delight in these experiences, but, as he says, while the

11. John C. Hodge, 'Perceptions of the Museum Environment', in *Museum Education in a Changing World*, MEAA Conference (Perth, August 1979), pp.121–9
12. P.E. Griffin and K.B. Start, 'Evaluation of Museum Education Services', in *New Directions in Museum Education*, Australian Unesco Seminar, Adelaide (March 1975), pp. 21–34
13. Kenneth Hudson, *A Social History of Museums: What the Visitors Thought* (London: Macmillan Press, 1975).

Museum of the College of Surgeons was undoubtedly capable of giving great pleasure to one small girl[14] this is probably not the same thing as saying that it was either a good or a successful museum, since it was not designed to give pleasure to small children.

Recollections by Dillon Ripley, who became Secretary of the Smithsonian Institution, show not only the delight of a child but also indicate the elements in these experiences which his successful professional career enabled him to identify. While living in Paris at the age of 10 he enjoyed opportunities for play in the gardens of the Tuileries, which alternated with periods of wandering and exploration in the galleries of the Louvre. Of these he writes:

> There was no essential difference in all this. The juxtaposition was natural and easy. No threshold of tiredness and lack of concentration was reached. It was as easy as breathing in and out. For children, then, museums should be infinitely easy, diverse, varied. There should be fun and games somewhere, perhaps just outside, and concentration and indirect learning inside, but there should be no real distinction between the two. The outside should flow into the inside, the inside out.[15]

A further important element was described by Sir Charles Fleming, formerly Chief Palaeontologist, Geological Survey, in a private discussion on aspects of museum display. In support of exhibits arranged to show the systematics or classification of animals, Sir Charles mentioned how useful these had been to him as a boy. With a pocketful of shells which he wished to identify, he used the classified arrangements in the public galleries of the Auckland War Memorial Museum until 'I found my way eventually into the back and met Powell (A.W.B. Powell, Assistant Director and Conchologist) and then I was right, for as long as he would put up with me'. Other instances of assistance on a personal basis by scientists in our museums would be useful to investigate, as it could well have been an important element in the effectiveness of our museums in the past few decades.

While visiting museums in Australia in 1979, we were surprised to be asked on two separate occasions to explain the source of our apparently high output of successful scientists in natural history, and this would be an interesting field of investigation. Certainly while working in the National Museum in the late 1950s one often became aware between 3.30 and 4 p.m. of quiet rustlings in the corridors of the staff quarters as children from the local high schools crept their way to the museum workrooms on a completely informal and personal basis. The need for security and changes in administration probably now prevent these encounters, and the needs of today's children may have to be met through the provision of well-thought-out facilities for leisure activities to meet differing levels of interest and development.

14. *Ibid.*, Mrs Shann at the Museum of College of Surgeons (in the Victorian era), p.89.
15. Dillon Ripley, *The Sacred Grove* (London: Victor Gollancz Ltd, 1970), pp.140-1.

Museums formerly placed more emphasis on recreational activities, particularly clubs for children, some of which, as in Auckland, held an annual camp as well as regular meetings and field trips. The Boys Conchology Club in Auckland was so successful that in 1934 it led to the formation of an adult Museum Conchology and Natural History Club. There is evidence of sustained interest with some former members developing careers in scientific areas from the long-running clubs in Auckland and Christchurch. In addition, there were special holiday displays, nature trails in the museum grounds, museum gallery trails, activity sheets and quizzes for use during the holidays. Quiz sheets, currently provided at some museums, can lead to the award of certificates of 'museum explorer' status for children on the successful completion of a series. Manawatu Museum runs courses in printing and museum conservation during school lunch breaks. Some education officers have worked staggered hours to experiment with programmes during holiday periods when attendance is greater, but all efforts have been spasmodic. Most do not regard the recreative aspects of museum work as their responsiblity.

The Junior Museum Club in Canterbury Museum, a long-standing club, is run by museum staff, and so is the Otago Museum's holiday programme for children, organized by John Darby, Assistant Director, and held annually during the September holidays. For several years it included a science workshop for secondary school students to introduce them to the museum's display and research work. Its Explorers' Week programme for 300-400 9-11-year-olds has run far longer and uses quiz sheets termed 'walkabouts', drawing exercises, dramatizations, and a programme including four lectures daily for a week, which is a demanding schedule. To cater for this number of children, all museum staff from the director down are involved, but not the education officers who are on holiday. The children not only enjoy it but return year after year to participate, about one-third of them coming from the country. It clearly meets an important need for children. At the end of their Explorers' Week they have been asked to complete questionnaires about what they enjoyed and what they would like to see established for their use. The plea for a place to which they can go after school and in the holidays to 'do things', to have their specimens identified, to get advice, to use a microscope, and so on, is in line with suggestions made by directors for over 50 years for the establishment of such centres.

In Australia, provision for leisure activities is given high priority and may include special holiday exhibits and activities associated with these displays, holiday courses for a week on specific subjects, daily film programmes and museum walkabout question booklets. These activities are the responsibility of the education officers. The core of leisure activities is often the education centre where laboratory and facilities for drawing, modelling, and so on, are

HALL of MARINE LIFE

Some of the children at a session of Explorers Week holiday programme at Otago Museum (Photo: John Darby).

provided. Such centres are used for adult groups in the evenings to such an extent that it is rare for any evening to be entirely free. A new development at the Australian Museum, Sydney, is a 'Drop-in' after-school programme from 4 p.m. run by two teachers with assistance at times from skilled craftsmen and naturalists. Emphasis is on activities, the recommended age is 7-13, and parents are welcomed. There is no restriction on the number of times that children can attend, and evaluation studies by a team from the Department of Sociology, University of New South Wales, has begun.

Provision for older children with specific interests in museum fields is currently provided in many other countries through science clubs which provide additional opportunities for investigation and often run field trips and excursions in the holidays. An example comes from Santiago, Chile, where Young Scientists Clubs are provided with meeting rooms, a special reference library and laboratory facilities, and have access to scientific and research staff. It is interesting to read that it is rare for members over 18 years old to continue membership. Upon entering university, they usually leave for a period, but later return, spontaneously, offering their services as instructors for the younger members.[16] Provision of clubs with special facilities, and access to scientific staff is an important contribution museums can offer to potential scientists.

Services for Groups with Special Needs

There are groups of children and adults with special needs as well as those for whom a learning situation which is not dependent on written language is desirable. As teaching skills and knowledge of the needs of these groups is needed, experimental work is required. Responsibility for trying out and evaluating different areas could be shared. More information is needed on:

(1) Children of low academic performance whose response to a museum visit is usually very marked.

(2) Children of high intelligence, as response to museum objects is usually heightened by the background knowledge of the observer.

(3) People with disabilities, for example, the blind, the physically and mentally handicapped, and the hospitalized.

(4) Prison inmates.

16. Grete Mostny, 'Children and the Natural History Museum, Santiago, Chile', in *Museum*, Vol. XXXI, No. 3 (1979), p.176.

(5) Senior citizens.

(6) Children from multi-racial groups where English may be a problem. Museums may well have a special responsibility to people whose cultural inheritance they hold.

Children of High Ability

At the Lopdell House Training Course, 28 August-1 September 1972, the possibility of developing suitable programmes for small groups of children with special needs was given fairly high priority. A high point in the week-long sessions was reached when work with a group of gifted children visiting the National Museum and the National Art Gallery, with the cooperation of the education officers at both institutions, was described by John Ritson, formerly education officer at the National Art Gallery and then lecturer at Wellington Teachers College. He also put into perspective many of the skills used by children in learning to 'read' three-dimensional material and the different possibilities of visual interpretations in expression, observation and appreciation.

The following year, programmes for children of high ability were recorded at three of the main museums. These appear to have ceased at the National Museum, but they are still recorded in annual reports from the Auckland War Memorial Museum. Such classes continue to visit the Canterbury Museum about three times a term under the guidance of their own teachers. A visit from one of these classes, largely directed by the children themselves, is described in Chapter 1. This method appears to be highly successful and could be the basis for further experiments.

In her paper Celia O'Malley stresses that more attention should be given to 'the *quality* of education in helping gifted children to achieve their potential and contribute to the future both theirs and ours'. She feels that their needs must be answered by a review of traditional teaching systems and, in this review, states that 'museums must press for the re-assessment of the role the museums might play in the development of learning and think anew about how we can use our collections in the way we want to and not as embellishments to the traditional system'.[17]

This work is undoubtedly of importance and could be the responsibility of one staff member for experimentation and evaluation. Materials not usually on

17. Celia O'Malley, 'Museum Education and the Gifted Child', in *Museums Journal*, London, Vol. 76 (2 September 1976), p.59.

public display might be made available by using photocopies of archival materials and duplicate or good quality reproductions for handling, enabling these children to work on research-type studies of a scientific or archaelogical nature challenging to their abilities.

Handicapped Children

Museum services for the handicapped are known to provide profound and enriching experiences for many people with disabilities, and the earliest services in New Zealand gave emphasis to such work. V.F. Fisher in his MA thesis, 'Analysis of the Educational Work in New Zealand Museums', [18] 1946, describes weekly visits of blind children in groups of 10-12 to the Auckland War Memorial Museum from 1931. These classes, conducted by Dr Robert Falla, used strategies with common but not often encountered objects such as a live rabbit together with a mounted specimen, an articulated skeleton and an assortment of rabbit bones from which they might understand something of its structure. Falla emphasized the need to provide experiences which could later be extended by the children in their own time.

Both Auckland and Canterbury had regular classes for children from the schools for the deaf.

Auckland also worked with psychologically disturbed adults. Both Mrs Olwyn Turbott, who in 1945-6 cooperated with the mental hospital authorities in their occupational therapy departments, and A.W.B. Powell, who in 1942-3 assisted in experiments with hospitalized American servicemen, were members of the museum staffs. Fisher describes the work of Powell in cooperation with Major Merrill Moore, a psychiatrist attached to the US Medical Corps, at two US field hospitals in Auckland. Powell and Moore distributed attractive tropical shells from the Solomon Islands (where most patients had served) to encourage interest and increase manipulation of damaged hands and fingers. They found the desire and effort needed to produce a trinket so successful that appeals had to be made to the public to augment the supply of suitable shells.

Canterbury Museum was the first to experiment with visits to the children's wards at the hospital.

Emphasis on these services has been reduced to occasional visits of children from the Correspondence School, cerebral palsy schools, homes of compassion and some hospital wards. Auckland War Memorial Museum records visits of blind and deaf children between 1973-7, but such services are peripheral to the needs of the more numerous school classes. During such visits the education

18. *Op.cit.*

officers tend to provide materials for use by the teachers who are more familiar with the children's needs. It would be useful to do more, and a body of published information is available. The Department of Education lists 2,097 children in special schools and school groups for the intellectually handicapped throughout the country in 1977. More attention is being given to the problems of the handicapped in museums, and references to seminars and papers on this subject may be found in the Select Bibliography, Appendix C.

It is possible that separate lessons for such children are of less importance than providing them with additional sensory experiences, which are also appropriate to normal people. The important thing is that the handicapped child should be included with normal children in classes using expanded facilities. Alison Heath, Education Officer, Directorate of Ancient Monuments and Historic Buildings, Department of the Environment, Great Britain, and an expert in work with the handicapped, suggests that in general it is better for disabled visitors to be as fully integrated as possible with ordinary visitors to the museum, making full use of all facilities, and that the best help museums can give to disabled people is by the general improvement of displays and facilities. In her article, 'Museums and Handicapped People', she states:

> It is interesting to note that in the places where handling tables were provided especially for the blind, although there has been an initial flood of interest resulting from good publicity, as the publicity has gradually been forgotten, so the number of blind visitors has decreased and the general public have taken over because they too enjoy and benefit from such special provision. [19]

Similar interest by sighted people in an exhibition for the blind with access to handling materials is mentioned in an evaluation report on an exhibition, *More Than Just a Look*, prepared by the Education Services, National Gallery of Victoria, Melbourne. These findings parallel those of Mrs Heath in the interest shown by sighted people, children and adults who explored the exhibits while wearing blindfolds, as well as the success of visits from sighted classes which included blind children. The report comments:

> One girl who has never seen is in our ordinary school. She has 40 classmates. Twenty of them accompanied her to the exhibition to 'see' the exhibition with blindfolds. She was totally at home in the exhibition and her classmates now have a new concept of what her life is like. At one stage she had a tremendously calming effect on one of her classmates who became confused and disoriented. [20]

It was reported at a seminar in Leicester[21] that, because of the difficulty experienced by blind people in getting to the museum there, exhibits were

19. Alison Heath, 'Museums and Handicapped People', in *AGMANZ News*, Auckland, Vol. 8, No. 3, August 1977, pp.16-19.
20. *More Than Just a Look*: Report of an Exhibition for the Blind. Education Services, National Gallery of Victoria, October-November 1978 (mimeo).
21. *Museums and the Handicapped*, Seminar, University of Leicester, Department of Museum Studies, 1975.

removed from the building to a more accessible place. Similarly, the National Gallery of Victoria records difficulties encountered by such people in climbing the stairs or taking the small circular lift, which many found terrifying, to reach an exhibition on the third floor.

Comments on a special exhibition for the blind entitled 'Touch'[22] by Georgina Christensen, Deputy Director, Taranaki Museum, also suggest that such exhibits, with an opportunity to handle and to hear about artefacts in the collection, appeal to the general visitor as well as to the handicapped. Although directed to the needs of the 170 blind or partially sighted people in Taranaki province, most of whom are elderly, this exhibition attracted over 5,000 visitors to the museum during the four weeks of the display.

22. Georgina Christensen, 'Touch', in *AGMANZ News*, Auckland, Vol. 9, No. 2 (May 1978), pp. 12-13.

'Touch' (Photo: Taranaki Herald).

To overcome the difficulties encountered in transporting severely handi-capped people to the museum, the Australian Museum in Sydney uses a 'Wandervan', a unique teaching resource developed to provide a 'museum experience' for handicapped children unable to attend lessons at the museum. Although vans to transport museum materials to outlying schools and districts are not unusual, the Wandervan is the only one directed towards services for handicapped children, senior citizens, convalescent patients, migrant groups, and so on. It has been operating on an experimental basis for two years and is shortly due for evaluation and review.

Multiracial Groups

Museums also hold the cultural inheritance of both the Maori people and those of the Pacific Islands, which imposes responsibility on them to use these for opportunities for cultural enrichment and racial identity. It is an area calling for expertise and deep sensibility on the part of the planners and is one urgently to be kept in mind for development in the larger museums, for example, the National Museum and the Auckland War Memorial Museum, whose collec-tions are extensive and are in centres where numbers of these people are located.

Few specially designed programmes have been prepared with this in mind, although lessons on aspects of Maori and Pacific Island life are a principal part of the repertoire of most museum programmes. One innovative effort planned for multiracial groups held at the National Museum is described by the educa-tion officer, John Christie, in his annual report for 1978 as follows:

> The education officers were instrumental in coordinating three programmes for workers from Todd Motors. The multiracial nature of the workforce has meant conflict between racial groups and a carefully structured programme involving Todd's personnel staff, museum ethnologists and education staff was put together to create a better understanding of cultural differences. The programme was so successful that similar programmes are likely to be built into all their staff training programmes.

During periods of redundancy, groups of factory workers were occupied in turn with special educational programmes. The museum ethnologists, using models reconstructing various evolutionary stages, described current theories on the evolution of man. Following discussion, there was free exploration of the galleries with emphasis on Maori and Pacific Island collections, with staff and volunteer guides available for consultation.

The district served by the Gisborne Museum and Art Gallery has a predo-minantly Maori population, and sensitivity to their feelings and traditions has enabled the part-time education officer, Mrs Barbara Allum, to pursue a course of teaching on Maori culture in a way which few Pakeha can emulate. The guiding force springs from a close relationship between Mrs Allum and a Maori *kuia* (female elder). Before the official opening of their new building, for example, a totally private and unpublicized ceremony was conducted to lift the *tapu* (religious restriction) both from the new building and from the historical artefacts which it would house, thus making these freely available to all Maori children who wished to examine them. During study activities, Maori customs relating to *tapu* are scrupulously observed. Similar rites have been exercised before the opening of the new museum at Porirua.

A student teacher teaching Maori string games to a group of children of varying racial origins (Photo: John Buckland).

8 Where to next?

Under the leadership of the Council of AGMANZ, New Zealand museums and art galleries are working on the resolution of a new policy for education. At its conference in Gisborne in 1979, a discussion paper centred on work with schools, for example, teaching in schools rather than in the classroom; larger displays and circulating exhibitions; people with special needs; voluntary activities with children; relationships with Maori and Polynesian children; re-establishment of teacher training schemes; and the question of the control of the education officers and whether this should be taken over by the museums themselves. Understandably, this widely ranging agenda was not fully covered and the discussion was summarized as follows:

> . . . most were in favour of control by the institution and most felt that the education officer should not just be concerned with children in school hours. Some of the new, wide-ranging programmes for education officers in art galleries were also mentioned.

> The education officers' group compared notes on individual practice and felt that it was desirable that all education programmes should involve the children's active participation. The group considered that guidelines could usefully be prepared for small museums wishing to set up education services. They also considered the area of continuing education to be most important.[1]

Discussion on the same papers, presented a second time at the conference in March 1980 in Wellington, culminated in the formation of an education committee to consider these and wider ranging educational responsibilities in more detail. A new and well-defined educational policy in its widest sense is urgently needed to give direction to the current efforts of both museums and art galleries. To date, the only nationally based attempt to achieve a wider communication with the public was the Carnegie-funded experiments in 1938-41, whose measures were designed to meet suggestions emanating from the museums and art galleries themselves. These measures, in addition to services to schools, are documented by McQueen.[2]

1. Warner Haldane, 'Art Galleries and Museums in the Community', in *AGMANZ News*, Auckland, Vol. 10, No. 2 (May 1979), pp.2-3.
2. *Education in New Zealand Museums, op.cit.*

Contemporary social demands are far removed from those of the 1930s. The impact of television has significantly affected the position of museums in our society; museums are proliferating at an amazing rate throughout the country; there is a widespread interest in arts and crafts; a deep concern for the environment; an affirmation of racial identity among the Maori population; a widespread demand for continuing education; a greatly enhanced value placed on many of the artefacts which museums hold and collect; changing methods of teaching children and the challenge of an escalating tourist industry. In relation to all of these, museums and art galleries hold an important and significant place in present-day society.

Factors operating against them are the unfavourable economic climate, the rising costs of a threatened system of transport, a shortage of trained staff, an absence of analysis about their visitors, and lack of information about our total museum resources. Those most recently established may hold collections relating to local history or industry. Apart from them, there are technological collections, some of which are expanding to a very large size; there are collections emanating from private enthusiasts or specialist groups; and there are historical cottages or houses or institutions specializing in local history and art, which often act as a local centre of culture, combined with teaching of arts and crafts. This varied and constantly changing pattern of museums will become clearer with the publication in 1981 of a much needed descriptive and illustrated survey of the Museums and Art Galleries of New Zealand compiled by Professor K. Thomson, Dean of the Department of Social Sciences, Massey University, carried out with the assistance of a grant from the QE II Arts Council and to be published by A.H. and A.W. Reed, with the help of Unesco.

Much of the leadership in the past came from the metropolitan museums, but, with the increasing and varied range of institutions, the Council of AGMANZ has assumed responsibility for this. Its close working relationship with the Department of Internal Affairs and its responsible and protective attitude towards local museums have already enabled it to provide assistance towards capital costs, building extensions, curatorial and conservation services for the protection of articles of national importance held by small museums with untrained staff, as well as improving the displays of those museums that have sought help in presenting local history and industries. To achieve this, exchanges of material related to local history have been encouraged between institutions. The paper, 'Museum Outside its Four Walls',[3] by R.K. Dell, classifies the metropolitan, provincial and local museums, and succinctly describes the methods found to extend and improve the services offered by local

3. 'Museum outside its Four Walls': Paper presented at the Unesco Regional Seminar on *The Adaptation of Museums in Asia to the Needs of the Modern World*, March 1979, Tokyo and Kyoto.

museums with the expenditure of relatively little money through the appointment to the metropolitan museums of Auckland, Christchurch and Dunedin of extension officers, paid through the Department of Internal Affairs.

Although the proliferation of museums and increasing attendances evince widespread interest in museum collections, there is also a grave threat to their existence in the increase in their numbers, because of their competing need for financial support. By whom are our museums owned and how are they funded? Only two museums, the National Museum and the National Gallery, are largely funded by the Government, with additional revenue from local bodies. Collections owned by government departments, for example, DSIR, may be open to the public on request. Most other museums, usually controlled by museum boards or committees, are financed in a variety of ways, for example, by a levy on public rates; by admission charges; by donations; by profits from souvenir trading or tourist charges; or are operated by voluntary labour. All are struggling and, at times, competing for finance, and few of those currently staffed by education officers could afford the cost of salaries should financial support from the Department of Education be withdrawn. Within the spectrum of museums, no common denominator of goals or direction is apparent. Museums develop in response to the strengths of their collections, the philosophy of their directors and that of their controlling bodies, with shifts of emphasis often occuring after staffing changes. The longer established museums have shown such shifts between tertiary education, research, conservation, display, and public relations. Few operate a vigorous education policy, and the tendency in the past 10 years in the larger museums has been for the education services for schools to operate with the minimum communication between them, and for such services to be the principal ones offered.

There appears to be a lack of awareness of the threat to the equilibrium of the financial support of our museums. It is generally taken for granted that each should be supported by its 'community', that is, the population within a stipulated radius of the museum. When this is examined, we see that the taxpayer may in reality be financially supporting several museums simultaneously. As the National Museum and National Art Gallery are largely government funded, all taxpayers contribute to their support. In return, these institutions accept responsibility for significant though largely unknown services throughout the country. Metropolitan museums, such as the Auckland War Memorial Museum, may, through government legislation, receive contributions from local rating throughout a wide provincial area, although the rate will be less as distance increases. Within this area, provincial museums such as the Waikato Art Museum may also be supported by local rating, while local museums, or museums with admission charges such as MOTAT, will again elicit financial support. The taxpayer may well ask what benefits he derives from these payments, particularly if he is not a dedicated museum visitor. Indeed, it is possible that even museum-minded people visit other museums, when travelling, to a much greater extent than they visit those at home. As Kenneth Hudson[4] points out, 'community' may be a misleading term. In an analysis of visitors to a museum in an English provincial town, 45 percent of its visitors could be termed local, 22 percent regional, 29 percent national, and 4 percent international.[4]

A sustained analysis of the origins and interests of visitors to our museums is a matter of urgency.

Most professional discussions on policy are gravely inhibited, and at times break down completely, because of financial stringency. The problem is world-wide, and the historical account of the fluctuating financial fortunes of the museums of America in relation to times of economic recession by Hudson[5] makes sobering reading. It is imperative that the taxpayer should realize that the museum exists for him, is something in which he can participate, and is not merely for an unseen group of intellectuals. It is necessary, as Findlay says, that the 'ordinary' man or woman must be convinced, as well as those whom they vote into power, not only of what museums are doing for the community but also of what they are poised to do,[6] and this leads us back to the educational function of museums. Museums in the United States, as Harry S. Parker III points out, are becoming used to a strange new breed of professionals proclaiming that education has the key role in the twentieth century museum — people who lay claim to a new expertise, not about objects but about people.[7] The basic difference, as Ayala Gordon points out, between the traditional curator and the educator in the museum is that one focuses his or her attention on the object, while the other focuses on the people who will view the object.[8] Without the object and the curator, museums would not come into existence. It is possible also that without the educator to relate the object to the people, their continued existence would be gravely threatened. It has been said that a great many museums, perhaps the majority, do not know what they are trying to do. They exist, so to speak, because they are there, and because there has so far been just enough money to stop them from closing. But they are becoming almost impossibly expensive to run, and if it becomes necessary to finance

4. Kenneth Hudson, *Museums for the 1980s: A* Survey of World Trends (Paris:Unesco, 1977), p.77.
5. *Ibid.*, pp.166-76.
6. Ian Findlay, *Priceless Heritage, op.cit.*, p.49. This chapter examines these problems in detail and contains useful educational goals for museums of different types, for example, art galleries, natural history, technology, and so on.
7. Harry S. Parker III, *The Training of Museum Educator:* Papers from the Ninth General Conference of ICOM, *The Museum in the Service of Man, Today and Tomorrow*, ICOM, 1972, pp.167-71.
8. Ayala Gordon, 'The Museum, Schoolchildren and Teachers', *op. cit.*, p. 144

'Participation and play are among the means the museum has at its disposal to orge interaction with the young visitor' Photo: John Darby).

them from public funds, their continued existence will ultimately depend upon political decisions.[9]

Only recently has it become respectable to regard education and pleasure as closely linked, both for children and adults, a change which is of immense

9. Kenneth Hudson, *Museums for the 1980s, op.cit.*, p.171.

importance to museums. Puritanism, as Hudson says, has had a long run for its money in museum education, which in the second half of the nineteenth century had a sternly disciplined flavour and made few concessions to human weakness.[10] Emphasis on education must not be confused with emphasis on formal pedagogy. Indeed, as Henri Rivière, Permanent Advisor to ICOM has emphasized, the pedagogical approach must be an open and original one, able to meet the varied requirements of children today, to help them understand the world around them, to find their place in contemporary society and inspire a world for tomorrow. Participation and play, freedom of choice and a multiplicity of possibilities are among the means the museum has at its disposal, to forge a new type of interaction with the younger visitor.[11]

It is the term 'interaction' on which museums need to ponder. At present they hesitate between a purely scientific presentation of their collections and one aimed at appealing to the average visitor, a conflict which needs to be resolved. As Ger van Wengen, President of the ICOM Committee for Education and Cultural Action points out, it is of the utmost importance that those responsible for presentation or display agree upon a definite strategy, determined mainly by their visitor's interests. However, such endeavours to arouse visitors' empathy by means of attractive displays come up against an obstacle that should not be underestimated — the fact that curators are more often inclined to attend to their scientific work for which they have been trained, than to display aspects intended for a wider public.[12]

Whenever we speak of the educational activities of museums there is a tendency to refer to the work of the teaching staff giving verbal instruction in the exhibition halls. Yet it is the exhibits themselves which are the principal vehicles of museum teaching, and the quality of museum display is its principal educational tool, a truth of which our museums show little or no awareness. Few of our museums regard the function of display as intimately related to education or realize that this is achieved only when there is interaction between the display and the onlooker. Museum display is a subject in its own right on which a voluminous body of opinion has been published. Always a subject of contention, which frequently becomes emotional, it has of recent years become a centre of acute pressure in the United States and Britain where, to the astonishment and dismay of the museums, the well-educated, prosperous people, which surveys have identified as being their most consistent visitors, are attacking them on this very question. What they are asking for, even demanding of their museums, is that their collections, which constitute

10. *Ibid.*, p.9.
11. Georges Henri Rivière, Editorial: 'Museums and Children', in *Museum*, Unesco, Paris, Vol. XXXI, No. 3 (1979), p.146.
12. Ger van Wengen, Introduction: 'Museums and Children', *Ibid.*, p.149.

material evidence, be displayed in a manner which relates to public issues of the day. While many writers comment on this, John Kinard, Director of the Smithsonian Institution's Anacostia Neighbourhood Museum summarizes the problem in relation to minority groups when he says:

> The great historical and scientific truths of the past mean nothing to the average man unless they are shown in relation to what is happening today, and what may happen tomorrow.

> It is the museum's responsibility to discover the truth, to collect and analyse the data and to interpret the findings in a way that all men can understand. The cultural contributions of minorities must be dealt with and understood. Because some society refuses to respect the black man, the red man and the brown man, there is no reason for museums to blank them out as though they did not exist.

> Exhibits should be designed to present these controversial problems side by side with their counterparts in history, correlating current issues with historical facts. Our museums should be the leaders in the forefront of change rather than following the dictates of past generations. [13]

In speaking of problems of interpretation, Duncan F. Cameron, an internationally recognized authority on the planning, development and management of museums, comments on aspects of physical and biological sciences and how these relate to museum visitors when he says:

> The rejection of the traditional museum and especially of many of our truly great art museums by those desperately concerned with social change, is on first consideration, enigmatic. Museum audiences are growing at impressive rates in many parts of the world ... and yet many artists, intellectuals, students in protest, minority groups and governmental agencies... identify us as dinosaurs, much too expensive to feed or even tolerate.

> Where we have attempted to interpret cultural heritage to minorities, it has too often been in terms of the majority culture. Similarly, where museums have turned their attention to current issues, they have too often preached too little, too late, and to the converted. And the liturgy is still in Latin. [14]

Central to these problems are social values which are transmitted through society and which are connected very directly with many of the most urgent problems of today. Yet, as Klaus von Dohnanyi points out, there is comparatively little debate about these values. He writes:

> The complexity of industrial life, its dependence on a nature-destroying industrial production are slowly becoming clear to us. Do we realize that the world we complain about is the world we have made ourselves? It is mankind which is making life on this earth more and more dangerous for mankind. And since there is nothing which man does which is not part of his education, we must also recognize that the industrial world which is beginning to threaten us is the product of our own values.

> Maybe rational concept of change is not to be expected because... articles,

13. John Kinard, 'Intermediaries between the Museum and the Community', in ICOM Conference papers, 1971, *op.cit.*, pp.151-6.
14. Duncan F. Cameron, 'Problems in the Language of Museum Interpretation', *ibid.*, pp.89-99.

speeches and statistics... have limited effect upon our basic attitudes and values. In my opinion, a new confrontation with nature, with aesthetics, with human history is required. Not only the rationale but the senses must be engaged. Even television, as important as its information qualities are, will never be a substitute for the three-dimensional reality.

The museum with its authenticity, where the time spent on certain objects is solely controlled by the visitor, the museum with its originality offers a particular opportunity for such a confrontation . . . and an important opportunity for human reflection.[15]

Are museums of these countries poised on the brink of participation in current social issues, and, if so, is this the role which lies ahead of our museums? At present it is unlikely that many could attempt such measures, even were its management bold enough to agree, because the only way in which such displays could be presented, and the institution survive its involvement with conflicting groups, would be as the result of professionally impartial research. Few of our museums have sufficient research staff to accept these challenges, but they could go much further than they do at present. Social and economic changes in our part of the world frequently follow upheavals in other countries, and the consequences of failing to communicate meaningfully with as wide a range of people as possible in our society cannot be ignored. The educational task of the museum is no longer simply to exhibit collections as they are, but to do its utmost to ensure that their message is deeply assimilated, and that its visitors are able to understand and feel what they see. Each object associated with man can provide an example of inventiveness and creativity, and its presentation should enable the visitor to visualize both the object and the manner of its production in the context of the social processes, or the period of time it represents. The ultimate aim is to bring the visitor, whether child or adult, into contact with a moment in the whole life of the past or the present in such a way that the image he receives will be compounded of present, past, future, nature and society, as in reality.[16]

It is therefore of great importance that the most careful consideration be given to the problems of the current services for children, the only body of visitors to our museums who are truly representative of our society. The needs of adolescents and adults, the interests of both museum-going people, and those who never enter its doors, should be deeply considered. The role museums may be called upon to play may well tax their resources to the utmost, and, to this end, help and cooperation should be sought from all other educational bodies. In this respect, the presence of the education

15. Klaus von Dohnanyi, 'The Third Dimension in Education; Chance and Task of the Museum', in ICOM Conference papers 1971, op.cit., pp.75-81.
16. Juan Gómez Millas, 'Museums and Lifelong Education', in Museum, Unesco, Paris, Vol. XXV, No. 3 (1973), pp.157-64.

officers in the museums should be seen as bridging the gap between museums and the formal education system, to be used eagerly as a means of strengthening their own educational philosophy and position. The current sources of friction between them are in no way due to measures which threaten the right of museums to determine their own educational identity, but appear in fact to be due to the intransigences of administration which have long been known as red tape. The traditional and time-honoured way to circumvent this is always personal encounter, and museums should seek a close-working relationship with the Department of Education as they do with the Department of Internal Affairs.

The white heron diorama at Canterbury Museum. Should museum exhibits show only undisturbed environments? (Photo: Canterbury Museum).

The question of taking over control of the education officers by the museums has been raised frequently, and over a long period. It is often difficult to see past immediate problems to anticipate other hazards which might be encountered by such a change, and discussions have not ranged much further than finance. Yet in the United States and Great Britain where many education officers are appointed directly to the museum staff, they face immediate problems of communication and of understanding between themselves and the complex and constantly changing school system which they wish to serve, and close-working relationships are neither easy to establish or to maintain. Our present arrangement brings to the services for schools the professional support and expertise of the education system at primary school level, directed through its most influential channels by the personal involvement of the DSIs at provincial level. When museums are able to examine and assess the resources they can allocate, closer links between the secondary schools and the teachers colleges could be sought in the same way. Strategies for continuing education at open university level and for adult education could also be approached through the education system.

Rather than take responsiblity for the education officers, each large museum should give urgent attention to the establishment within its staffing structure of its own education department, headed by a professional museum educator with curatorial status. Education officers, who are teachers trained for work at different levels within the educational system, would work as a team within this department, which should have wide-ranging responsibilities.

The appointment of a curator of education as recommended by the ICOM Working Party on Training of Museum Educators (Appendix A, No. 2) and by Dr Alan N. Baker of the National Museum in his ANZAC Fellowship Report 1974-5 is urgently needed. It would immediately solve some existing problems and provide a means of encouraging further extensions, with seconded or appointed teachers at primary and secondary school levels. A curator of education would be able to:

(1) Participate at curatorial level in planning permanent displays and temporary exhibitions.

(2) Provide better communication with the Department of Education by being outside the hierarchy of the education system.

(3) Take responsiblity for research on aspects of museum education and of museum visitors.

(4) Coordinate and develop services for primary and secondary schools.

(5) Facilitate an increased use of museum resources for training student teachers.

(6) Establish leisure activities.

(7) Promote educational programmes at adult level.

(8) Provide advisory services for small local museums for their educational problems.

(9) Develop and evaluate different types of extension work.

The needs of our own people, children and adults for more meaningful communication in museums also apply to the significantly large, and often totally unconsidered group of visitors to our museums who are tourists. In the past decade, the number of overseas visitors coming to New Zealand has increased from 155,000 to 420,000, representing an average annual increase of 10.5 percent.[17] The dramatic increase in tourism is a world-wide phenomenon, which has materially affected museums everywhere. As Grete Mostny, Chairman of the ICOM National Committee points out:

> A vigorous cultural tourism has sprung up [since the Second World War] that brings to museums an international public which is eager to know other people, other cultures, other ways of life. This cultural and scientific tourism signifies also a spontaneous step towards regional, continental and world integration. Among the chief attractions and 'musts' for tourists, museums enjoy a high priority, serving for the mutual comprehension of people and influencing favourably the economy of their countries.[18]

A few of our museums are supported and even thrive on this industry, by admission charges, sales of souvenirs and additional charges, with opportunities for visitors perhaps 'to pan for gold', to ride in a vintage vehicle or to play an outmoded musical instrument. Yet our principal museums largely ignore the busloads of tourists decanted through their doors, except to count their numbers. Unless the sociable bus driver attempts to explain exhibits to them, their enforced and strictly limited time is unstructured. Certainly, when the time is short, and the background and interest of the tourists is unknown, little may be accomplished. As Dr Zygulski, of the Institute for Philosophy and Sociology of the Polish Academy of Sciences, points out:

> Research shows that the average member of a large party of tourists has very limited possibilities of taking in what is shown; the speed with which the visitors are taken round, the inadequacy of their basic information on the question, the difficulty they have in following the explanation given, their lack of interest in the subject of the exhibition, and so on, combine to prevent them from assimilating the contents of what they see.[19]

17. *Museum News,* MOTAT (Inc.), Auckland (June 1980), p.3.
18. Grete Mostny, 'The Function and Aims of Museums', in ICOM Conference Papers, *op.cit.,* (1971), p.33.
19. Kazimierz Zygulski, 'The Museum and the Adult', in ICOM Conference Papers, *op.cit.* (1971), pp.125-36.

Main hall of Maori exhibits, National Museum. No provisions is made to introduce tourist groups to the collections (Photo: National Publicity Studios).

Tourists outside the organized groups often fare better and frequently spend more time in our museums. Should we not use this opportunity to aim directly at providing better understanding of ourselves and of the unique aspects of our nation's natural and cultural heritage? Within the large museums most generally patronized by tourists, shouldn't displays be prepared and direct efforts made to communicate with international visitors about our culture, our traditions, the past and present relationships of our racial and cultural groups, and of our unique flora and fauna, to help them to a better appreciation of our way of life?

The majority of our museums are small[20] and the wide-ranging responsibilities suggested here might well appear to them to be a counsel of perfection. It may be all they can do to keep the building weatherproof and the collections safe. Yet the importance and the significance of the small local museum must be emphasized. It often brings to its 'community' a sense of identity, an affirmation of its historical and cultural heritage. As Findlay points out, without such backgrounds the quality of life is unsatisfactory. The small museum, if expanded, can become the focus for the effort to discover identity.[21] It can become a meeting place for groups interested in arts and crafts, local or natural history or an aspect of technology related to a local industry. To visit a small museum may be to survey a largely incomprehensible collection of junk, but it may also be rewarding. These museums are usually established and maintained by voluntary enthusiasts. The drive

20. Rose Cunninghame, 'The Needs and Importance of Local Museums', *AGMANZ News*, Auckland, Vol. 8, No. 2 (May 1977), pp.13-15.
21. Ian Findlay, *Priceless Heritage, op.cit.*, p.172.

A few of our museums are supported and even thrive on the tourist industry. Panning for gold at Shantytown Museum, Westland (Photo: National Publicity Studios).

which motivates them to collect and care for these collections on an unpaid basis also sustains these efforts against the continued pressures of everyday management and lack of finance. Their enthusiasm and their helpfulness in showing visitors their treasures, explaining their history and significance, may provide the personal guidance missing in the larger museums and often communicates a valuable measure of their own interest and delight.

Some musems which have sought assistance from the metropolitan extension officers, for example, Waihi Museum, have been able to increase useful local collections, in this case, related to gold mining. Its displays, including excellent working models of gold-mining processes made by one of its volunteer committee, its well-presented historical gaols and thought-provoking artefacts, vividly portraying something of the hardships of the early miners, are an interesting record of local development. As we have already pointed out when commenting on single visits to museums, it is a pity that help or advice about handling class visits is not provided for these museums.

Despite limited staffing, some of the local or smaller provincial museums contain models of communication, although, unfortunately, we have not been able to visit many of these. The provincial museum of Southland, for example, experiments with artefacts provided for the casual visitor's personal examination. By noting changes in the positions of these artefacts, the staff gains some idea of their apparently frequent handling by visitors. Despite lack of supervision, only one exhibit has been lost over a number of years. Of special interest is a three-dimensional exhibit on caves, whose principal objects are so cunningly placed that they impart a sense of discovery to the curious visitor who succeeds in finding them.

The Coaltown Museum, Westport, uses auditory tapes triggered by an electronic beam to transmit the sounds of manually operated coal mining, when a visitor enters its replica mine. The audible but tantalizingly indistinguishable conversation of the simulated miners holds the visitor in the darkened exhibit long enough to begin to feel something of the atmosphere of a mine. Similarly, the simple but dramatic exhibit of a laden coal truck poised at the steepest angle of the Denniston Incline arouses feelings of apprehension as the visitor approaches. The labels and tapes of information about the Incline, which was the only access to the settlement for miners and their families, help the visitor, when standing beside this restrained force, to imagine something of the courage and fortitude of these people.

These and many other exhibits provide museum experiences which are thought-provoking and therefore memorable. Beyond all doubt, the key to communication in the museum depends in the end on the right people who possess the power of alchemy to change for someone else a heterogenous collection of objects into a treasure house of wonder.

Artefacts provided for the personal examination of the casual visitor at Arrowtown Lakes District Centennial Museum (Photo: National Publicity Studios).

Tapes of manually operated coal mining establish an atmosphere of realism in this replica coal mine. Coaltown Museum, Westport (Photo: National Publicity Studios).

Appendix A

Recommendations of ICOM Working Party on Training of Museum Educators, 1969[1]

1. New attitudes in education are steadily replacing the formal, conceptual approach to learning which has dominated so much teaching in the past. Today there is an increasing awareness of the need to encourage methods of individual inquiry and the study of original source material. The teaching structure is becoming a joint venture in learning between child and teacher, and similar changes are taking place in adult education.
2. Education in the museum reflects this change in attitude. Until recently, it fulfilled a passive role; today, due in part to pressures and demands made by an ever-increasing number of visitors, the whole concept of education in the museum is changing. Former traditional methods of talks, lectures and display no longer suffice. Its role has become more complex and includes problems of administration as well as modern techniques of communication. To meet these new requirements and to carry out an effective cultural and educational programme, the Working Party recommends: that a department of education be set up within the existing structure of the museum in charge of a curator, keeper or educator, according to the terminology used.
3. The work of this department is as specialized as that of other departments in the museum. Its first concern is to establish close and satisfactory communication between the public and the exhibits within and out of the museum (loan services, temporary exhibitions, clubs, etc.). To this end, the curator or educator must be trained to identify the different categories of visitors, understand their motives in coming to the museum and satisfy their needs.

1. From *Pterodactyls and Old Lace*, *op.cit.*, pp.69-70.

4. He must cooperate with other cultural and educational bodies of school age and be able to initiate the use of documentary and audio-visual media relating to the objects. To carry out this work effectively, the department should have premises specially equipped and a staff trained to achieve these objectives.

5. The Working Party accordingly recommends that the training of the educationalist in the museum should include the following subjects:

   (1) Techniques of communication (to achieve contact with the object by verbal, visual, and practical media).

   (2) Evaluation of the different categories of the museum public (the casual visitor, the specialist visitor, the scholastic public, etc.).

   (3) Knowledge of up-to-date teaching methods and modern developments in education in relation to the museums.

   (4) Certain aspects of museology, in particular, problems of display in permanent collections, in temporary and circulation exhibitions and in loan services.

   (5) Administration including financial matters.

   (6) The administrative structure of educational and cultural institutions with which he will cooperate.

   (7) Activities within and without the museum (clubs, field studies, etc.).

   (8) The preparation of educational material for specific use with different categories of the public.

Suitable training for students, teachers, and museum staff is basic to the development of educational activities in museums. Interesting pilot work has been done by individuals but it is now a matter of urgency that institutions should coordinate their interests and plan together.

Appendix B

Withdrawal of Student Teachers from Museums

The working relationship between museum education services and teachers colleges had been close and apparently satisfactory for many years. Both organizations assumed that any changes following the introduction of Three Year Training would be the outcome of an official assessment of the value of this work. The absence of an explanation, other than the announcement of a general reduction in the total number of days which students might spend in the schools, was baffling. In the *Report of the Commission on Education in New Zealand*,[1] used as a blueprint for the establishment of this training, museums are not mentioned.

The records of the Department of Education in 1969 contain annual reports of education officers who commented unfavourably on the effects the withdrawal of students was having on class visits, and these have been carefully annotated. Special reports on these effects were requested by the Director-General from all the DSIs whose districts were affected, but surprisingly, these reports are not on file. As the museums were also concerned about these changes, the Council of AGMANZ requested the Director-General of Education to allow a senior officer to attend their conference in Wanganui in March 1969 to discuss the situation. J.M. Wiseley, DSI, Wanganui attended, and it is possible that the reports from the other DSIs were sent to him beforehand for reference.

A detailed account of the conference is held in AGMANZ records and we are grateful to their secretary, Captain John Malcolm, for supplying an account of this meeting. The administrative changes and the new autonomy of the teachers colleges were described by Mr Wiseley who pointed out that museum training and full cooperation were not prevented between these institutions. It

---

1. Commission on Education in New Zealand, *Report of the Commission on Education in New Zealand* (Currie Report) (Wellington: Government Printer, 1962).

was now a matter of negotiation between each college and the museums. However, training was possible on only a limited number of weeks each year and was largely confined to second-year students. The problems this posed the museums by its limitation of their programmes were not resolved. No evaluation of the quality of museum training was mentioned.

We are grateful to Allan S. Mackie, formerly Principal, Wellington Teachers College, for answering some of the questions which have troubled museum directors and education officers. As he pointed out, some of the success of the 1960s was more apparent than real. The expanding numbers of students entrusted to the museums for training had been useful to colleges whose roll numbers strained the facilities of cramped, outdated buildings. The introduction of Three Year Training was linked to the construction of new and more spacious buildings throughout the country. Until these were ready, pressures of accommodation forced colleges to send students out into schools for a greater proportion of their time. Once the colleges were in the new buildings, this time would have been reduced. The annual growth in attendance figures, as we have pointed out in Chapters 2, 4, actually reflected the rising rolls of the schools. The quality of the service provided by the museums was never discussed, because the transfer of the education officers to the staffs of the normal schools had removed museums from the responsibility of the colleges. Thus, they were not included in the brief for consideration when planning took place.

Continued use of museums by the colleges has been due mainly to the efforts of college staff members who had previously had museum sections and who devised ways of sending students to the museums at intervals. This shows that they regarded museum training as a useful means of learning teaching techniques and that their own experience appears to have had laid the foundations for a relationship which had lasted many years.

The number of students being trained at present is climbing slowly (see Table A7), although the period of three weeks is not altogether satisfactory. No students are sent to Otago Museum, but Palmerston North Teachers College now posts one or two students at a time to both Manawatu and Wanganui Museums. Between 1938-77, 8,500 students are recorded as having had between 16-24 days training in a museum. As the records are not complete for all institutions, the actual total would probably be about 9,000, of which about 150 were secondary teachers college students (Tables A6, A7).

Appendix C

Select Bibliography

The literature of museology and museum education is enormous. Those who wish to read further will find a significant change in technical and philosophical ideas since about 1960, although these changes have been more rapid in some countries than in others. Publications before that date are now of interest mainly in the tracing of the growth of ideas.

A useful basic list of periodicals, series, bibliographies, books and articles may be found in *Museums for the 1980s: A Survey of World Trends* by Kenneth Hudson, published by Unesco, Paris 1977, pp.180-4. This lists 26 titles under The Educational Work of Museums. A wider ranging list of 139 titles on museum education since 1970, prepared by the Unesco-ICOM Documentation Centre, Paris, in collaboration with Stella Westerlund may be found in *Museums and Children: Monographs on Education,* ed., Ulla Keding Olofssen, Unesco, Paris 1979, pp.183-95. Bibliographies in the books and articles listed provide opportunities for further extension. The major museum periodicals listed by Hudson, especially *ICOM News,* report new publications promptly.

Books

Bay, Ann, *Museum Programmes for Young People:* Case Studies (Washington, DC: Smithsonian Institution, 1973).

Bazin, Germain, *The Museum Age* (New York: Universe Books, 1967).

Beaumont, H.W. *Educating in Five Dimensions,* Reeds Practical Handbooks for Teachers (Wellington: A.H. and A.W. Reed, 1960).

Borum, Minda, *Measuring the Immeasurable: A Pilot Study of Museum Effectiveness* (Washington, DC: Association of Science — Technology, 1977).

Communications Design Team of the Royal Ontario Museum, *Communicating with the Museum Visitor:* Guidelines for Planning, Part A: *Education and Learning* (Toronto: Royal Ontario Museum, 1976), pp.17-24.

Cresswell, John, *The Museum of Transport and Technology of New Zealand* (Auckland: Paul Hamlyn, 1976).

Department of Education and Science, *Museums in Education:* Education Survey No. 12 (London: HMSO, 1971).

Dixon, Brian, Courtney, Alice, and Bailey, Robert, *The Museum and the Canadian Public/Le Musée et le public canadien* (Toronto: Government of Canada, 1974).

Fairley, John A. *History Teaching Through Museums:* Education Today Series (London: Longman Group Ltd, 1977).

Findlay, Ian, *Priceless Heritage: The Future of Museums* (London: Faber and Faber, 1977).

Goldman, Katherine J., ed., *Opportunities for Extending Museum Contributions to Pre-college Science Education:* Summary Report of a Conference supported by the National Science Foundation (Washington, DC: The Smithsonian Institution, 1970).

Greenaway, Frank, et al., *Science Museums in Developing Countries* (Paris: ICOM, 1962).

Group for Educational Services in Museums, *Museums and the Handicapped*, Seminar, Leicester, September 1975 (University of Leicester, Department of Museum Studies and Adult Education, 1975).

Group for Educational Services in Museums, *Museum School Services* (London: Museum Association, 1967).

Hands-on-Museums: Partners in Learning: A Report from Educational Facilities Laboratories, New York, NY (Educational Facilities Laboratories, 1975).

Harrison, Molly, *Changing Museums: Their Use and Misuse*, Longman's Education Today Series (London: Longman, Green and Co., 1967).

Harvey, E.D. and Friedberg, B., eds, *A Museum for the People:* A Report of Proceedings at the Seminar of Neighbourhood Museums, November 1969 (New York: Arno Press, 1971).

Hudson, Kenneth, *A Social History of Museums: What the Visitors Thought* (London: Macmillan Press, 1975).

Hudson, Kenneth, *Museums for the 1980s:* A Survey of World Trends (Paris: Unesco, 1977; Macmillan, London).

International Council of Museums (ICOM), Committee for Education, *Museums and Teachers* (Paris: ICOM, 1956).

ICOM, *Training of Museum Personnel/La formation du personnel des musée:* Published with the help of the Smithsonian Institution, Washington, DC (London: Hugh Evelyn for the International Council of Museums, 1970).

ICOM, Working Party on Kits, *Kit, What is that?* (Stockholm: Riksutställningar, 1973).

Larrabee, Eric, ed., *Museums and Education:* Papers from a conference held at the University of Vermont, August 1966 (Washington, DC: Smithsonian Institution Press, 1968).

Marcousé Renée, *The Listening Eye:* Teaching in an Art Museum, Victoria and Albert Museum (London: HMSO, 1961).

McCabe, G.I., ed., *Education through Museums:* A Bibliography (London: Group for Educational Services in Museums, 1972).

McQueen, H.C., *Education in New Zealand Museums:* An Account of Experiments Assisted by the Carnegie Corporation of New York (Wellington: NZCER, 1942).

Mills, John Fitzmaurice, *Treasure Keepers* (New York: Doubleday, 1973).

Morley, Grace, *Museums in South, Southwest and East Asia:* A Review and Report, ICOM Regional Agency in Asia, 1967-1977/ICOM Regional Agency in Asia (New Delhi, 1977).

Museums and Handicapped Students: Guidelines for Educators (Washington, DC: Smithsonian Institution, 1977).

Museums, Imagination and Education: Museums and Monuments XV (Paris: Unesco, 1973).

Oliver, Ruth Norton, ed., *Museums and the Environment:* A Handbook for Education (Washington, DC: American Association of Museums, 1971).

Olofssen, Ulla Keding, ed., *Museums and Children:* Monographs on Education (Paris: Unesco, 1979).

Parr, Albert Eide, *Selected Papers, 1959-1967, Bibliography, 1926-1967* (New York: American Museum of Natural History, n.d.).

Pitman, Bonnie L., *Watermelon*, Weisner Wing Training Notebook, revised (New Orleans: New Orleans Museum of Art, 1975).

Ripley, Dillon, *The Sacred Grove:* Essays on Museums (London: Victor Gollancz, 1969).

School Council Publication, *Pterodactyls and Old Lace:* Museums in Education (London: Evans Brothers and Methuen Educational, 1972).

Screven, C.G., *The Measurement and Facilitation of Learning in the Museum Environment* (Washington, DC: Smithsonian University Press, 1974).

Smyth, Bernard W., *The Role of Culture in Leisure Time in New Zealand:* Series: Studies and Documents on Cultural Policies (Paris: Unesco, 1973).

Stevens, R.A., *Out-of-school Science Activities for Young People* (Paris: Unesco, 1969).

Wengen, G.D. van, *Educatief werk in musea* (Groningen, H.D. Tjeenk Willink, 1975).

Winstanley, Barbara, *Children and Museums* (Oxford: Basil Blackwell and Mott, 1967).

Wittlin, Alma S., *The Museum, its History and its Tasks in Education*, International Library of Sociology and Social Reconstruction, ed. Dr Karl Mannheim (London: Routledge and Kegan Paul, 1949).

Wittlin, Alma S., *Museums: In Search of a Useable Future* (Mass. and London: MIT Press, 1970).

Wohler, J. Patrick, *The History Museum as an Effective Educational Institution* (Ottawa: National Museums of Canada, 1976).

Zetterberg, Hans L., *Museums and Adult Education* (Augustus Kelly for the International Council of Museums, 1969). Published with the help of Unesco.

Conference Papers

ICOM, *Museum Contributions to Education:* First Australian ICOM Seminar, Melbourne, 1971. Australian National Committee for the International Council of Museums.

ICOM, *The Museum in the Service of Man, Today and Tomorrow:* Ninth General Conference of ICOM, Paris and Grenoble, August-September 1971. (Paris: ICOM, 1972).

MEAA, *Museum Education Training:* Conference of Museums Education Association of Australia, Sydney, April 1966.

MEAA, *Museum Education in a Changing World:* Conference of the Museums Education Association of Australia, Perth, August 1979.

Unesco, *International Symposium on Museums in the Contemporary World:* Final Report, Paris, 1969.

Unesco, *New Directions in Museum Education:* Australian National Committee for Unesco, Adelaide, March 1975.

Unesco, *Regional Seminar on the Adaptation of Museums in Asia to the Needs of the Modern World.* Tokyo and Kyoto, March 1976.

Unesco, *Round Table on the Development and the Role of Museums in the Contemporary World:* Santiago de Chile, Chile, May 1972, Unesco, Chile, 1972.

Unesco, *The Role of Museums in Education:* Australian National Advisory Committee for Unesco, Sydney, 1966.

Unpublished Thesis

Barrow, T.T.., 'A Survey of the Organization and Administration of Education in the New Zealand Museums and Art Galleries', MA thesis, 1954 (Victoria University of Wellington).

Dearnley, G.G., 'An Evaluation of Some Aspects of the Educational Value of the Dominion Museums School Service in Wellington City Area', MA education thesis, 1947 (Victoria University of Wellington).

Fisher, V.F., 'An Analysis of the Educational Work in New Zealand Museums', MA education thesis, 1946 (Auckland University).

Hall, J.C., 'School Loan Cases and Problems of their Distribution in New Zealand with Special Reference to the Dominion Museum', thesis for the Diploma of the Museums Association, Great Britain, 1954.

Scott A.W., 'School Children and the Museum', MA education thesis, 1952 (Auckland University).

Articles

Alpers, Anthony, 'High Praise for our Museums', in *Home and Building*, April 1956.

Anderson, Duane, C., 'Project ETW: An Exemplary School-museum Program', in *Curator*, New York, Vol. 16, No. 2 (June 1973), pp.141-57.

Bannister, J.L., 'Co-ordination of Educational Services in Local Museums', in *Museum Contributions to Education:* First Australian ICOM Seminar, Melbourne, 1971.

Bark, Lois, 'Museum Experience for the Exceptional Child', in *Museum News*, Washington, DC, Vol. 46, No. 2 (October 1967), pp.33-5.

Bartlett, J.E., 'Museums and the Blind', in *Museums Journal*, London, Vol. 54, No. 11 (Feburary 1955), pp.283-7.

Beardsley, Don G., 'Helping Teachers to use Museums', in *Curator*, New York, NY, Vol. 18, No. 3 (September 1975), pp.192-9.

Bunning, Richard L., 'A Perspective on the Museum's Role in Community Adult Education', in *Curator*, New York, NY, Vol. 17, No. 1 (March 1974), pp.56-63.

Burch, Glenn, E. and Ulland, Linda M. 'Learning by Living', in *Museum News*, Washington, DC, Vol. 55 No. 1 (September-October 1976), pp.23-31.

Cameron, Duncan F., 'How Do We Know What Our Visitors Think?', in *Museum News*, Washington, DC, Vol. 45, No. 7 (March 1967), pp.31-3.

Cameron, Duncan F., 'A Viewpoint: The Museum as a Communications System and its Implications for Museum Education', in *Curator*, New York, NY, Vol. 11, No. 1 (1968), pp.33-40.

Chase, Richard A., 'Museums as Learning Environments', in *Museum News*, Washington, DC, Vol. 54, No. 1 (September-October 1975), pp. 37-43.

Christensen, Georgina, 'Touch', in *AGMANZ News*, Auckland, Vol. 9, No. 2 (May 1978), pp.12-14.

Condit, Louise, 'Children and Art', in *Museums, Imagination and Education: Museums and Monuments, XV* (Paris: Unesco, 1973), pp.61-82.

Coon, Nelson, 'The Place of the Museum in the Education of the Blind', American Foundation for the Blind, Education Series No. 6, New York, NY, 1953.

Cooper, R.C., 'The Role of Museums in Education in New Zealand', in *The Role of Museums in Education: Australia Unesco Seminar* (Sydney), 1966.

Cox, Peter, 'The Museum and Youth', in *The Museum in the Service of Man, Today and Tomorrow:* Ninth General Conference, ICOM, 1971 (ICOM, Paris, 1972), pp.137-43.

Dell, R.K., 'Museum Outside its Four Walls', Paper presented at Regional Seminar on the Adaptation of Museums in Asia to the Needs of the Modern World, March 1976, Tokyo and Kyoto.

Dohnanyi, Klaus von, 'The Third Dimension in Education: Chance and Tasks of the Museum, in *The Museum in the Service of Man, Today and Tomorrow:* Ninth General Conference, ICOM, 1971 (ICOM: Paris, 1972), pp.75-81.

Eyles, Alan M., 'Museums and Adult Education', in *WEA Review*, Wellington (October 1970), pp. 124-6.

Findlay, Ian, 'What Image, What Public?', in *Museums Journal*, London, Vol. 64, No. 3 (December 1964), pp.248-53.

Fine, P.A., 'The Role of Design in Educational Exhibits', in *Curator*, New York, NY, Vol. 6, No. 1 (1963), pp.37-44.

Gabianelli, Vincent J. and Munyer, Edward A., 'A Place to Learn', in *Museum News*, Washington, DC, Vol. 53, No. 4 (December 1974), pp.28-33.

Ghose, Shri S.K., 'Museums and Scientific Knowledge', in *Museums in the Service of Man, Today and Tomorrow:* Ninth General Conference, ICOM (ICOM: Paris, 1972), pp.49-62.

Gómez Millas, Juan, 'Museums and Lifelong Education', in *Museum*, Paris, Unesco, Vol. 25, No. 3 (1973), pp. 157-64.

Gibbs-Smith, Charles H., 'The fault . . . is . . . in ourselves', in *Museums Journal*, London, Vol. 64, No. 3 (December, 1964), pp.226-33.

Gordon Ayala, 'Ten Years of Work in the Youth Wing', in *The Israel Museum News*, Jerusalem, No. 11 (1976), pp.27-34.

Gordon, Ayala, 'The Museum, Schoolchildren and Teachers', in *The Museum in the Service of Man, Today and Tomorrow:* Ninth General Conference, ICOM, 1971 (Paris: ICOM, 1972), pp.144-50.

Grant, Anne Cox, 'Broader Horizons for the Handicapped', in *Museums Service*, Rochester, Vol. 29 (March 1956), p.37.

Griffen, P.E. and Start, K.B., 'Evaluation of Museum Education Services', in *New Directions in Museum Education:* Australian Unesco Seminar, Adelaide (March 1975), pp.21-34.

Haldane, Warner, 'Art Galleries and Museums in the Community', *AGMANZ News*, Auckland, Vol. 10, No. 2 (1979), pp.2, 3.

Hale, John, 'Museums and the Teaching of History', in *Museum*, Paris, Unesco, Vol. 21, No. 1 (1968), pp.67-72.

Hansson, A., 'Blindness: A Personal Experience': Contribution to Seminar on *Museums and the Handicapped*, University of Leicester, 1975.

Haskell, S.H., 'The Mentally Retarded Child: Classification, Learning Difficulties and Training Strategies', in *Museums and the Handicapped*, University of Leicester, 1975.

Haydock, Stephen, 'Teachers and Teacher Trainees', in *Museum Education Training:* MEAA Conference, Sydney (April 1977), pp.23-4.

Heath, Alison, 'Excursions to Museums, Sites and Monuments as Sources of Knowledge', in *Museum*, Paris, Unesco, Vol. 31, No. 3 (1979).

Heath, Alison, 'Museums and Handicapped People', in *AGMANZ News*, Auckland, Vol. 8, No. 3 (August 1977), pp.16-19.

Heath, Alison, 'The Training of Education Officers', in *Museum Education Training:* MEAA Conference, Sydney (April 1977), pp.5-9.

Hodge, John C., 'Existing Education Officer Training Programmes', in *Museum Education Training:* MEAA Conference, Sydney (April 1977), pp.10-15.

Hodge, John C., 'Preliminary Evaluation of Classes visiting the Australian Museum, in *Museum Education in a Changing World:* MEAA Conference, Perth (August 1979).

Hudson, Kenneth, 'Learning Stations, Customized Work Sheets and Exhibit Effectiveness: The New Museum Jargon', in *Museums Journal*, London, Vol. 75, No. 4 (March 1976), pp.165-6.

Hume, T.A., 'Museums and Education in the United Kingdom', in *The Role of Museums in Education:* Australian Unesco Seminar, Sydney, 1966.

Hume, T.A., 'The Role of Museums in Education', in *The Role of Museums in Education:* Australian Unesco Seminar, Sydney, 1966.

Hunt, Glenn and McLeod, Janet, 'Museums: A Community Resource for the Handicapped', in *Museum Education Training:* MEAA Conference, Sydney (April 1977), pp.25-31.

Hubendick, Bengt, 'Museums and the Environment', Paper read at the Ninth General Conference, ICOM, *The Museum in the Service of Man, Today and Tomorrow*, Paris and Grenoble, August-September 1971 (Paris: ICOM, 1972), pp.39-48.

International Council of Museums, 'Conclusions of a Symposium on the Educational and Cultural Role of Museums', organized under the auspices of ICOM, Paris, November 1964: Appendix A in *Museums and Adult Education* by Hans L. Zetterberg.

Jelinek, Jan, 'The Modern, Living Museum', in *Museum*, Unesco, Paris, Vol. 27, No. 2 (1975), pp.52-9.

Kinard, John, 'Intermediaries between the Museum and the Community', in *The Museum in the Service of Man, Today and Tomorrow:* Papers of the Ninth General Conference of ICOM, Paris and Grenoble, August-September 1971 (Paris: ICOM, 1972), pp.151-6.

Koslov, G., 'The Joint Educational Activities of the Polytechnical Museum in Moscow', Appendix B, in *Museums and Adult Education*, by Hans L. Zetterberg (1969), pp.49-54.

Kurylo, Lynne, 'On the Need for a Theory of Museum Learning', in *Gazette*, Ottawa, CMA/AMC, Vol. 9, No. 3 (1976), pp.20-4.

Lefroy, J.A., 'Museums and Educational Institutions', in *Museums Journal*, London, Vol. 67, No. 2, pp.158-60.

Luca, Mark, 'The Museum as Educator: Annotated Bibliography of the Growth of an Idea', in *Museums, Imagination and Education: Museums and Monuments*, XV (Paris: Unesco, 1973), pp.148-8.

Manawatu Museum Staff, 'An Exhibition Concept for Participant Education', in *AGMANZ News*, Auckland, Vol. 11, No. 1 (February 1980), pp.12-14.

Marcousé, Renée, 'Animation and Information', Appendix D, in *Museums and Adult Education* by Hans L. Zetterberg (1969), pp.57-62.

Marcousé, Renée, 'Changing Museums in a Changing World', in *Museums, Imagination and Education: Museums and Monuments*, XV (Paris: Unesco, 1973), pp.17-21.

Markham, S.F. and Oliver, W.R.B., 'A Report on the Museums and Art Galleries of New Zealand to the Carnegie Corporation of New York' (London: Museums Association, 1933).

Matthai, Robert A. and Deaver, Neil E., 'Child-centered Learning', in *Museum News*, Washington, DC, Vol. 54, No. 4 (March-April 1976), pp.15-19.

McDonald, Patricia M., 'An Assessment of the Results of Museum Educational Programmes', in *The Role of Museums in Education*, Australian Unesco Seminar, Sydney (1966).

McDonald, Patricia M., 'A New Approach to Loan Collections: The Australian Museum, Sydney', in *Museum* (Paris: Unesco, 1972), Vol. 24, No. 4.

Mesallam, Mahmoud Hassan, 'The Exhibitions a Developing Country Needs', in *Museums, Imagination and Education: Museums and Monuments, XV* (Unesco: Paris, 1973), pp.113-22.

Morris, Graham C., 'The Child and the Museum', in *Museum Education Training: MEAA Conference*, Sydney (April 1966), pp.16-18.

Mostny, Grete, 'Children in the Natural History Museum', in *Museum* (Paris: Unesco, 1979), Vol. 31, No. 3.

Mostny, Grete, 'The Functions and Aims of Museums', in *The Museum in the Service of Man, Today and Tomorrow: Ninth General Conference of ICOM*, Paris and Grenoble, August-September 1971 (Paris: ICOM, 1972), pp.31-8.

Neill, Shirley Boes, 'Exploring the Exploratorium', in *American Education*, Vol. 14, No. 10 (December 1978), pp.6–13.

Oliver, W.R.B., 'New Zealand Museums: Present Establishment and Future Policy', Dominion Museum, Wellington, New Zealand, 1944.

O'Malley, Celia, 'Museum Education and the Gifted Child', in *Museums Journal*, London, Vol. 72, No. 2 (September 1976), p.59.

Olofssen, Ulla Keding. 'Temporary and Travelling Exhibitions', in *Museums, Imagination and Education: Museums and Monuments, XV* (Paris: Unesco, 1973), pp.91-103.

Park, G.S. 'The Diploma of the Museums Association', in *AGMANZ News*, Auckland, Vol. 9, No. 2 (May 1978), p.16.

Parker III, Harry S., 'The Training of Museum Educators', in *The Museum in the Service of Man, Today and Tomorrow: Ninth ICOM General Conference*, Paris and Grenoble, August-September 1971 (Paris: ICOM, 1972), pp.167-71.

Parker, Harley W., 'The Museum as a Communications System', in *Curator*, New York, NY, Vol. 6, No. 4 (1963), pp.350-60.

Parr, Albert Eide, 'Museums and Realities of Human Existence', in *Museum News*, Washington, DC, Vol. 45, No. 4 (December 1966), pp.24-9.

Proctor, D.V., 'Museums — Teachers, Students, Children', in *Museums, Imagination and Education: Museums and Monuments, XV* (Paris: Unesco, 1973), pp.23-9.

Razgon, Abraham, 'Museums and Multidisciplinary Universal Education in the USSR', in *Museum* (Paris: Unesco, 1976), Vol. 28, No. 1, pp.28-33.

Read, John, 'Television and the Museum', in *Museums, Imagination and Education: Museums and Monuments, XV* (Paris: Unesco, 1973), pp.83-90.

Ramsay, G.R., 'Education in the Seventies', in *Museum Contributions to Education: First Australian Unesco Seminar*, Melbourne, 1971.

Ripley, Dillon, 'Museums and Education', in *Curator*, New York, NY, Vol. 11, No. 3 (1968), pp.183-9.

Rivière Georges Henri, Editorial: 'Museums and Children', in *Museum* (Paris: Unesco, 1979), Vol. 31, No. 3, p.146.

Royston, Olive, 'A Visit to New Zealand', in *Museums Journal*, London, Vol. 57, No. 10 (January 1958), pp.231-3.

Szpakowski, André, 'Collaboration between Museum and School', in *Museums, Imagination and Education: Museums and Monuments, XV* (Paris: Unesco, 1973), pp.133-43.

Taylor, Anne P., 'Children and Artifacts — A Replacement for Textbook Learning', in *Curator*, New York, Vol. 16, No. 1 (March 1973), pp.25-9.

Thomas, W. Stephen, 'How Do Museums Use the Mass Media?': A Report from the United States, in *Museums, Imagination and Education: Museums and Monuments, XV* (Paris: Unesco, 1973), pp.123-31.

Thomas, W. Stephen, 'The Museum as a Communicator': Appendix E, in *Museums and Adult Education*, by Hans L. Zetterberg, pp.63-72.

Thomson, J. Allan, 'Some Principles of Museum Administration Affecting the Future Development of the Dominion

Museum': Appendix to the Journals of the House of Representatives of New Zealand, Vol. III, 1915.

Turbott, E.G., 'The Auckland War Memorial Museum — Its Place in the Community', in *Recreation in New Zealand*, Vol. 11, pp.72-4, Auckland Regional Authority, 1972.

Varine-Bohan, Hugues de, 'The Modern Museum: Requirements and Problems of a New Approach', in *Museum* (Paris: Unesco, 1976), Vol. 28, No. 3, pp.130-43.

Verrall, R.J., 'Tasmanian Museum and Art Gallery — Travelling Museum Project', in *AGMANZ News*, Auckland, Vol. 8, No. 3 (August 1977), p. 9.

Vigtel, Gudmund, 'Child's Work', in *Museum News*, Washington, DC, Vol. 55, No. 1 (September-October, 1976), pp.32-5.

Washburn, Wilcomb E., 'Do Museums Educate?', in *Curator*, New York, NY, Vol. 18, No. 3 (September 1975), pp.211-18.

Waterman, Stafford M., 'International Year of the Child: North Shore Teachers College Students on Teaching Section at the Museum of Transport and Technology', in *AGMANZ News*, Auckland, Vol. 10, No. 2 (May 1979), pp.7-8.

Waterman, Stafford M., 'Museums as Educational Partners', in *AGMANZ News* Auckland, Vol. 8, No. 2 (May 1977), pp.21-4.

Wells, Barry, 'Museum Education as I See it: A Personal Viewpoint', in *Museum Education in a Changing World:* MEAA Conference, Perth, (August 1977), p.9.

Weiner, George, 'Why Johnnie Can't Read Labels', in *Curator*, New York, NY, Vol. 6, No. 2 (1963), pp.143-56.

Wengen, Ger van, 'Introduction: Museums and Children', in *Museum* (Paris: Unesco, 1979), Vol. 31, No. 3, p.149.

Whitaker, J.H. McD., 'Geology for the Blind', in *Museums Journal*, London, Vol. 65, No. 4 (March 1966), pp.299-300.

Wilson, J.L.J., 'Museums and Adult Education', in *The Role of Museums in Education:* Australian Unesco Seminar, Sydney, 1966.

Zygulski, Kazimierz, 'The Museum and the Adult', in *The Museum in the Service of Man, Today and Tommorrow:* Ninth ICOM Conference, Paris and Grenoble, August-September, 1971 (ICOM, 1972), pp.125-36.

Appendix D

Table A1   *Total School Attendances at Four Main Museums 1948-77*

Year	Otago	Canter-bury	National Museum	Auck-land	Totals	% of National School Rolls*
1977	50,000	50,808	23,500	46,513	170,821	22.63
1976	50,000	45,020	30,000	52,902	177,922	23.56
1975	53,300	45,009	28,000	51,791	178,100	23.90
1974	52,000	44,892	29,000	62,920	188,812	25.78
1973	56,980	44,951	29,957	58,384	185,315	25.57
1972	42,000	42,179	20,000	58,936	163,115	22.72
1971	38,726	44,756	13,079	59,384	155,945	21.96
1970	36,000	49,179	13,591	53,034	151,804	21.55
1969	32,400	44,791	20,642	64,110	161,943	23.17
1968	30,000	33,316	13,467	64,428	140,470	20.36
1967	25,000	41,799	15,549	56,313	138,661	20.71
1966	29,000	44,687	14,711	39,806	128,204	19.95
1965	33,000	44,806	13,187	42,306	133,299	21.11
1964	25,000	48,614	16,171	34,278	124,063	20.14
1963	20,000	38,318	17,915	41,584	117,817	19.67
1962	18,000	33,609	15,088	37,077	103,774	17.83
1961	24,500	30,873	17,431	30,642	103,446	18.39
1960	27,310	31,502	20,731	41,234	120,777	22.16
1959	31,050	31,257	18,414	30,226	110,947	21.09
1958	30,100	30,000	17,614	27,730	105,444	20.84
1950	33,406	31,102	8,500	29,020	102,028	29.02
1948	23,487	36,000	1,500	29,031	90,018	25.65

*Taken from E-1 Annual Reports of the Department of Education to the House of Representatives.

Table A2   *Auckland War Memorial Museum Attendance Records, 1940-77*

Year	Primary	Intermediate	Post-Primary	Totals
		School Attendance		
1977	32,458	7,546	6,509	46,513
1976	33,777	12,424	6,701	52,902
1975	33,831	9,670	8,290	51,791
1974	38,850	12,680	8,216	62,920
1973	39,222	13,243	5,919	58,384
1972	37,468	14,812	6,656	58,936
1971	48,770	6,383	4,231	59,384
1970	40,985	6,635	5,414	53,034
1969	48,286	9,906	5,918	64,110
1968	47,253	11,211	5,964	64,428
1967	44,079	6,555	5,679	56,313
1966	32,525	3,606	3,675	39,806
1965	35,990	4,240	2,076	42,306
1964	25,656	4,935	3,687	34,278
1963	36,198	2,428	2,958	41,584
1962	31,676	2,674	2,727	37,077
1961	25,693	2,519	2,430	30,642
1960	31,903	5,023	4,308	41,234
1959	25,947	1,017	3,262	30,226
1958	21,298	2,394	4,038	27,730
1957	24,822	2,773	3,370	29,965
1956	25,640	1,278	2,992	29,910
1955	19,973	3,266	3,178	26,417
1954	28,606	3,752	4,199	36,557
1953	21,234	3,827	5,372	30,433
1952	22,094	8,030	3,966	34,090
1951	20,899	3,171	5,028	29,098
1950	22,162	5,128	1,730	29,020
1949	17,822	3,786	4,288	28,598
1948	20,769	4,262	3,760	29,031
1947	16,723	3,801	3,040	23,564
1946	16,830	6,774	7,694	31,298
1945	—	5,808	10,067	38,610
1944	—	—	—	16,211
1943	—	—	—	15,211
1942	—	—	—	12,575
1941	—	—	—	10,661
1940	—	—	—	14,838

Table A3   *Primary, Intermediate and Post-Primary Attendances at Auckland War Memorial Museum, 1960-77*

Year	Primary Pupils	% Primary National Roll	Interm. Pupils	% Interm. National Rolls	Post/Pry Pupils	% National Post/Pry Rolls
1977	32,485	8.19	7,546	6.06	6,509	2.81
1976	33,777	8.58	12,424	9.61	6,701	2.91
1975	33,831	8.64	9,670	7.33	8,290	3.77
1974	38,850	10.00	12,680	9.54	8,216	3.94
1973	39,222	10.08	13,243	10.15	5,919	2.92
1972	37,468	9.56	14,812	11.17	6,656	3.37
1971	48,770	12.36	6,383	5.22	4,231	2.22
1970	40,985	10.28	6,635	5.67	5,414	2.90
1965	35,990	9.82	4,240	4.01	2,076	1.31
1960	31,903	9.87	5,023	5.01	4,308	3.61

Table A4   *Primary, Post-Primary and Total Attendances at Canterbury Museum, 1960-77*

Year	Primary	% of National Primary Rolls	Post/Pry	% of National Post/Pry rolls	Total Attendance	% of Total School Rolls
1977	36,963	7.10	4,666	2.01	50,808	6.73
1976	33,221	6.35	4,581	1.99	45,020	5.96
1975	31,595	6.04	5,211	2.37	45,009	6.04
1974	32,517	6.24	5,005	2.40	49,892	6.81
1973	30,677	5.90	5,649	2.78	44,951	6.02
1972	30,488	5.88	3.722	1.89	42,179	5.87
1971	33,077	6.40	3,584	1.88	44,756	6.30
1970	36,633	7.11	3,194	1.71	49,179	6.98
1965	34,526	7.31	3.168	2.00	44,806	7.10
1960	28,289	6.68	565	0.47	31,257	5.73

Table A5   *Analysis of Booked Visits in Pupil-Hours to Auckland War Memorial Museum by Class and Area, 1975*

Area	Post-Pry	F2	F1	S4	S3	S2	S1	Infants	Totals
Colonial	220[1]	475	903	1,023	183	170	87	—	3,061
Studies	451[2]	68	1,581	349	155	148	50	64	2,866
	316[3]	146	672	153	130	248	34	123	1,822
Maori	399	12	46	355	467	1,259	1,326	58	3,922
Court	393	72	—	978	2,036	2,795	1,680	389	8,343
	381	237	418	1,205	2,908	1,270	1,246	621	8,286
Hall of	481	177	492	56	32	45	210	89	1,582
Man	137	34	189	103	179	753	720	190	2,305
	1,013	234	488	178	155	177	701	157	3,103
Pacific	96	84	—	—	45	180	—	—	405
Court	85	18	258	248	78	119	114	30	950
	364	81	21	40	441	330	48	60	1,385
Earth	288	125	—	24	39	—	105	—	581
Sciences	90	280	240	186	140	123	142	39	1,240
	154	164	240	58	48	—	—	—	664
Bird	60	30	—	156	142	121	227	74	810
Hall	—	—	—	—	157	125	137	343	762
	—	—	59	17	226	264	385	70	1,021
General	1,183	145	247	413	172	45	66	100	2,371
Visits	213	102	403	104	47	106	179	50	1,204
	548	181	71	342	100	200	89	—	1,531
Maritime	—	129	262	476	56	16	—	—	939
Hall	—	24	—	17	17	—	—	70	128
	—	—	6	—	94	—	—	—	100
Furniture	687	60	51	105	12	—	—	—	915
Hall	70	—	—	—	—	—	—	—	70
	—	—	—	—	—	—	—	—	—
Other	390	—	22	90	—	28	28	—	558
Areas	214	—	—	36	—	—	—	—	250
	57	71	52	143	48	60	186	—	617
Totals	3,804	1,237	2,023	2,698	1,148	1,864	2,049	321	15,144
	1,653	598	2,671	2,021	2,809	4,169	3,022	1,175	18,118
	2,833	1,114	2,027	2,136	4,150	2,549	2,689	1,031	18,529
Grand Total									51,791

Key: 1 = First Term; 2 = *Second Term;* 3 = Third Term

Table A6 *Student Teacher Postings to Auckland War Memorial Museum, 1950-77*

Year	Auckland		North Shore	Post-Primary	Totals
1977	25		19	1	45
1976	26		21	0	47
1975	13		20	1	34
1974	9		26	0	35
1973	26		40	0	66
1972	+		+	+	31
1971	+		+	+	46
1970	+		+	+	28
1969		75		5	80
1968		46		6	52
1967		99		6	105
1966		79		6	85
1965		88		6	94
1964		93		9	102
1963		112		5	117
1962		+		+	111
1961		+		+	117
1960		+		+	114
1959		+		+	95
1958		+		+	110
1957		+		+	115
1956		+		+	119
1955		+		+	96
1954		+		+	96
1953		74		3	77
1952		120		18	138
1951		111		10	121
1950				Posted for first time. Figures not stated.	

+ Figures not stated.
No returns appear for Ardmore College.
Third Year Training was phased in in 1968.

Table A7   *Number of Student Teachers Trained at the Four Main Museums, 1948-77*

Year	No. of Students Trained	Attendance at 4 Museums
1977	121	170,821
1976	121	177,922
1975	100	178,100
1974	122	188,812
1973	98	185,315
1972	147	163,115
1971	142	155,945
1970*	325	151,804
1969	301	161,943
1968	219	140,470
1967	262	138,661
1966	437	128,204
1965	432	133,299
1964	443	124,063
1963	425	117,817
1962	375	103,774
1959	411	110,947
1951	304	103,435
1949	194	102,028
1948	251	90,018

* Last of Otago

Appendix E

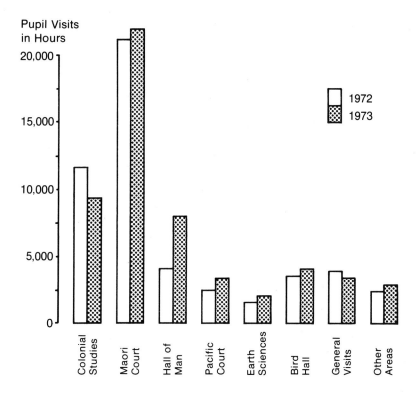

Figure A1 *Bar Graph Showing Total Use of Areas in the Auckland War Memorial Museum, 1972-3*

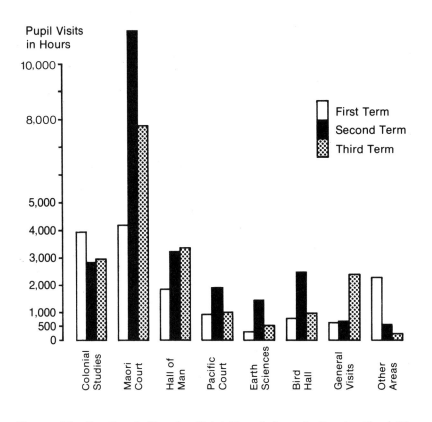

Figure A2 *Bar Graph Showing Total Use of Areas in the Auckland War Memorial Museum, 1973*

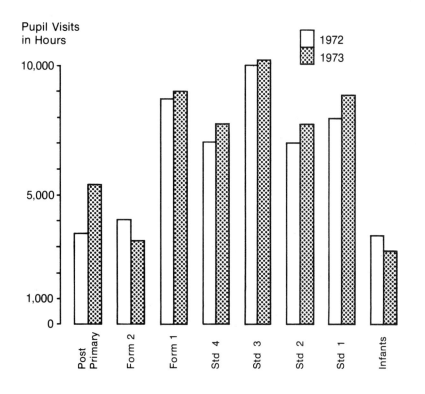

Figure A3 *Bar Graph Showing Use by Classes of Auckland War Memorial Museum, 1972-3*

Index